MW00967152

The Basics:
Nailing Down
What Builds You Up

The
BASICS

Nailing Down
What Builds You Up

MARK LITTLETON

Christian Publications
Camp Hill, Pennsylvania

Dedicated to:

Rich and Kathy Starsoneck
and the staff and members of New Horizons:
without your help, living–let alone writing–
would not be possible

Christian Publications
3825 Hartzdale Drive, Camp Hill, PA 17011

The mark of ✝ vibrant faith

ISBN: 0-87509-549-6
LOC Catalog Card Number: 93-74751
© 1994 by Mark Littleton
Cover and interior art © Ron Wheeler
All rights reserved
Printed in the United States of America

94 95 96 97 98   5   4   3   2   1

Unless otherwise indicated, Scripture taken from
the HOLY BIBLE: NEW INTERNATIONAL VERSION®.
© 1973, 1978, 1984 by the International Bible Society.
Used by permission of Zondervan
Publishing House. All rights reserved.

CONTENTS

" This Is a Football!"

Vince Lombardi, the famed football coach for the Green Bay Packers and later the Washington Redskins, mastered many motivational methods. During one locker room "chew-out" session, he proclaimed that his men were playing poorly. Why? Because they didn't know the fundamentals of the game.

At the next team meeting, Lombardi stood up before his players holding their game ball. He said, "Gentlemen, today we start getting back to the basics. This"–and he held up the pigskin in his hand–"is a *football!*"

After the laughter subsided, he went on to teach his team what he considered the fundamentals–the basics–of playing the game. That team went on to win several national championships.

To play any game, to succeed at any task, to reach any worthy goal requires *knowledge*–and the ability to use that knowledge well. It's no different with Christian faith and living. Any person who wants to know the Lord, serve Him, follow Him and worship Him must understand the truth about Him, His world and His people. If you don't know the rules, you can't play effectively. If you don't understand what the goal is, how can you head for it? If you don't know why the other players are there, how can you gain the cooperation that is so essential to success?

Centuries ago, Christians were "Lone Rangers." Some sat on pillars. Others roamed in the desert and lived alone in caves. Many joined monasteries.

But Jesus never intended for Christianity to be a solitary activity. It's a team effort. It requires tremendous skill to make it work. Anyone anywhere can start at any point and move forward. Christ meets us where we are. From there, He takes us to where He wants to get us.

I became a Christian in August 1972. It was an emotional, life-wrenching, immensely personal experience. He stopped my hellbent pursuit of pleasure, drugs, sex and the next "high" and turned me into a virtual fanatic against all those things when used illicitly. Jesus became all that mattered. Pleasing Him and knowing Him was the passion of my life.

Few members of my family understood what had happened to me. Here I'd gone from this happy-go-lucky, go-for-the-gusto college guy to this crazy preacher determined to get everyone he met to "trust Christ." It's not that I ceased to enjoy life or that I was against the world's basic pleasures. Quite the contrary, I discovered that all legitimate pleasures were even better. Ice cream ceased to be just ice cream. Rather, it was "a shot of electric thrill on my taste buds," or so I described it in my "waxing lyrical" moments. A kiss and romance weren't simply a means to get to second base, but a tingling prelude to greater joys in marriage. Everything in life suddenly seemed bigger, better, more beautiful than they ever had in my B.C. ("before Christ") days. It was a welcome and jubilant transformation.

But I had one problem: I didn't know anything. For awhile, I wasn't even sure who Jesus was. I knew He was God incarnate. But I didn't know what "incarnate" meant. Nor was I sure how His "God-ness" and His "human-ness" intersected. Where did God end and human start? Was Jesus like me in any way? Or was He more like Superman?

Gradually, I found answers to those questions as I attended church, read my Bible, prayed and fellowshiped with others. Getting those fundamentals down was difficult. Everyone had a different recipe. One told me to have "a quiet time every day." I thought that meant to be quiet, and I figured I could do that fine asleep as well as conscious!

Others counseled me to get involved in church in everything I had time for. This soon led to one tired puppy. I had no idea the church featured that many programs. And here I thought it all happened between eleven a.m. and noon on Sunday.

Still others exhorted me to do evangelism and lead "the lost" to Christ. I was already doing that–with little success–as I buttonholed every old friend and crammed the "good news" down his gullet. It wasn't going well. The gullets were big to begin with, and there were beer cans already stuck in them!

What to do?

Get back to the basics. Suck down some fundamental truths, begin applying them and then let God lead.

It wasn't that complicated. I soon discovered that as I learned some new habit or "tool" for Christian living, my appreciation of life rocketed. I grew spiritually, and more things in life fell into place. The "adventure" that had begun when I met Jesus Christ only got better.

That doesn't mean everything was perfect. Today I look back and shudder to recall some of the trials I went through. But I shudder more to think of having to go through the same troubles without Jesus, or without knowing those fundamentals. They preserved me through some perilous times.

In this book, then, I hope to give you that foundation–to get you started and keep you moving in a real walk with Christ. Sinking down such roots cannot lead to anything less than the true adventure Jesus intends to make of all of our lives.

CHAPTER 1

Starting with Jesus

Monday:

Good News

There are times when I sure can use some good news.

For instance, some time ago I took my car in for its 70,000-mile checkup. The engine was emitting a low bumping noise, and I wanted that checked out as well as having all the other normal procedures done. The shop performed the work. I went in to pick up the car and received a bill for $637. I choked, then paid–by credit card. No wise American goes without one!

However, that little problem continued to

clunk away. What was it? I made an appointment to take the car back in. The night before, though, the engine began clanking so badly as I drove home that I knew something was desperately wrong. I tried to reach the service station, but the car coughed out about a half mile away. I sat there seething in anger, then pounded the steering wheel in frustration. "Lord, why did this have to happen?" As if God was going to write it in the sky!

Then I got down to negotiations. "This better not cost more than $2,000, Lord, or Your name is . . ."

I stopped there, realizing the sugar treatment would be better. "Please, Lord, please don't let it be more than $2,000." I thought it was transmission trouble.

A tow truck hauled my car back to the service station and the next day they said it was internal engine trouble–big bucks. They couldn't fix it. I had the car towed to another shop where they soon informed me, "It's going to be between $2,500 and $3,500."

I was aghast, but always one to look for the better deal, I began calling around. There were no better deals, only worse ones. "$3,000," one said. "$3,500," said another. I said, "Lord, this stinks."

Yes, I was angry. Bitter? You bet. Disgusted? Definitely. I really needed some good news. Like, "Guess what, Jesus touched your engine and now it's healed! *Hee-allled!* For free, no less!"

No such luck, though. That afternoon at work I turned on my radio. It just so happened that an ad came on advertising engine repairs. It said if I mentioned that ad, they'd take a 100 bucks off the final bill. I figured I had nothing more to lose except my credit cards. So I called them and, lo and behold, the man on the phone said they could put in a new engine for under $1,900. I was amazed. God had come through. Rack up another one for the "Big Guy"!

Good news! Don't you like to get that kind of news?

"It's a healthy boy!"

"You just won the nine-million-dollar Publisher's Clearinghouse Sweepstakes!"

"Guess what, we're going to Hawaii! And Dad's paying all the bills!"

"Yes, I *will* marry you! I *will!*"

Take a minute right now. If you could have any piece of good news come your way this very minute, what would it be? Why do you think the gospel is called good news? Is it good to you?

THE EXTRA MILE

Take a look at these passages about some good news for all of us:

2 Timothy 1:7
Galatians 5:22-23
John 10:10
John 3:16
1 Corinthians 15:3-4

Tuesday:

Who's Lost?

Have you ever been lost?

Really lost, like in the woods with some bozo who can't find the trail, it's getting dark, and there are beasts out there making horrific hungry noises?

Really lost, like down a blind alley in the inner city, with a gang of thugs hiding among the trash cans, looking to take your wallet and have some fun with a gun?

Home Alone it isn't. Being lost can be terrifying. The feeling of being lost–having no idea which way to go–can be even worse.

When I graduated from college with a degree in Physical Sciences (Math/Chemistry/Physics, not Phys. Ed., please–no offense to you Phys. Ed. dudes out there, but it's not for me), for the first time in my life I had to make it on my own. Dad said to me, "Now you're on your own, kid. Go to it!"

Yo! Like where, man? I didn't have a clue. I wasn't a Christian then and I had no sense of "God's *decent* plan for my life," let alone a *wonderful* one. It was more like, "It's sink or swim, Buddy, and you look like you just had rocks for lunch." I was deeply and psychically frightened. I had to "do something" with my life, but what? I remember well that feeling of the vast unknown–getting a job, getting married, buying a house, having kids–it looked like a monster mountain I had to scale bare knuckled and ropeless. A cliffhanger it was!

What made it worse was how so many of my friends just seemed to know what they wanted to do. One planned to be a neurological surgeon. Another, a corporate tax lawyer. A third, a barfly (or should I say, bar *thug*; but skip him). How could anyone be that specific? I wasn't sure I even wanted to be alive, but here were people who had it all sketched out–and home videos to prove it!

I felt lost.

Oh, I wouldn't admit that. "Oh, yeah, I'm going to be a doctor."

That was what I told people. But in my heart, I didn't want to be a doctor. I couldn't face four more years of the raw grind. Moreover, I just couldn't imagine giving people shots, having them strip in my office and then looking into runny noses all day.

I felt lost in another way, too. It concerned life in general, and death in particular. What was out there? What happened when you died? Was there a God? If there was, who was He? Could anyone know Him?

I figured if there was a hell, I was going there. I didn't even need a ticket. One look at my record and I was outta here!

What was worse, no one seemed to have any answers. For many of my friends it was a non-issue!

"Who cares about that stuff?"

"Don't sweat it, Littleton, no one knows the answers to those questions."

Have you ever felt lost–in your heart and soul? Scared? Worried?

No? Not even a tad overwhelmed? Never?

Well, take a look at some Scriptures anyway.

THE EXTRA MILE

What do these Scriptures say to you about the thought of being lost, either emotionally or spiritually?

Matthew 11:28-30
John 14:6
John 14:1-3
Isaiah 53:6

Wednesday:

What Is Faith?

"Gospel" is an Old English word. It was actually spelled, "godspell," meaning "good tale." We usually translate it "good news."

Paul summarized the gospel in First Corinthians 15:3-4: "For what I received I passed on to you as of first importance: that Christ died for our sins according to the Scriptures, that he was buried, that he was raised on the third day according to the Scriptures."

The gospel that Christians preach is this:

1. Christ died for your sins.
2. He rose from the dead.
3. Believe it, and you'll be forgiven and you'll live forever, too.

Pretty amazing, don't you think? All you need do is believe it. That is, believe your sins were placed on Christ and believe that He rose again on your behalf, and you receive eternal life and eternal forgiveness. You don't have to do anything. You don't have to try to change your ways. You're not required to perform a series of great feats to impress Him. You needn't give a certain sum of money to charity to "get in." You don't even have to attend church for a day or a month or a year before He'll say, "Okay, I'll take you."

You don't have to do a thing except believe.

How can that be? Is God crazy? Eternal life and complete forgiveness just for believing it's true?

Well, first of all, for most people that's not that easy. Some feel it's too simple. Others say it's not enough–God would require more. Still others say it leads to indifference. Once you've believed, there's nothing more to do. You could lead a life of sin anyway, knowing it's already forgiven.

People say such things because they don't understand what it means to "believe." To believe in Christ is not just an intellectual exercise–He did this, I do that and presto, I'm in!

No, real belief means heart, soul, mind and might belief. You put everything you are and have into this thing. For instance, take a guy who loves baseball. We could say he "believes" in baseball. What does he do? He thinks about baseball. He goes to the games. He reads books about it and he collects memorabilia. His belief changes him. Instead of watching *Roseanne*, he goes to a game. Instead of spending his money on jewelry or a fancy car or fixing up his house, he spends it on baseball. His whole life revolves around the sport.

That's the kind of belief we're talking about here. Anything less is not the real thing.

THE EXTRA MILE

Take a look at some of the things Jesus said to those who believed in Him:

Mark 1:17
John 8:32-34
John 6:33-35
John 6:66-69

Thursday:

Repent–of What?

When you hear the gospel explained by some people, they might mention repentance. They say you must "repent of your sins and believe in Christ," or something like that.

The issue of repentance and the gospel is rather controversial these days. Leading pastors and scholars say repentance is not necessary. Others say it is. What is the truth? Let me offer you my own view on the subject:

Paul says in Acts 26:19-20 as he speaks before King Agrippa, "So then, King Agrippa, I was not disobedient to the vision from heaven. . . . that they should repent and turn to God and prove their repentance by their deeds." Paul's gospel involved repentance and a "turning" to God.

Jesus told the Pharisees when they complained about Him dining with tax collectors and sinners, "I have not come to call the righteous, but sinners to repentance" (Luke 5:32).

John the Baptist said to those who came to him for baptism, "Produce fruit in keeping with repentance" (Matthew 3:8).

And Peter, on the first day the gospel was ever preached, told the Jews what they should do in light of Christ's death and resurrection:

"Repent and be baptized, every one of you, in the name of Jesus Christ for the forgiveness of your sins" (Acts 2:38).

The truth is that repentance and faith cannot be divided up. Repentance is the flip side of faith, and vice versa. If you believe in Jesus, you'll repent, too, because you can't be a friend of Jesus and love sin. And if you repent–change your mind about sin–you will certainly also have believed in Him.

Some people begin with the repenting side of their walk with Christ. I remember feeling deep conviction of sin for nearly nine months before I ever truly believed in Christ. When I did believe, though, I began repenting of all sorts of things like drugs, premarital sex, drunkenness and so on.

Repenting and believing go together. Neither is a static, one-time thing. Both are "now" things. "I believe" is a statement of things as they are "now." A better way to say it might be, "I have believed, I am believing and I continue to believe in Christ." By the same token, you will repent day by day of new and different sins as the Spirit reveals them to you. I'm continually finding something new I have to repent of!

Resist getting into long arguments about which comes first, repentance or faith. Both are part of following Christ. The closer you get to Him, the more you will repent, and the more you repent, the stronger your faith will become.

THE EXTRA MILE

What do these passages command us to do in relation to Christ?

John 6:40

Acts 16:31

Matthew 10:38-40

Friday:

How Do I Know It's True?

One of the first questions anyone who decides to follow Christ will face is, "How does anyone know all of these stories and statements in the Bible are true?" How can I be sure the Bible is right about all it says?

You will probably struggle at times with these questions all your life. But here's some ammunition for resolving the basic issue. First, just read the Bible to see what it says. Many people who speak of "contradictions" and "problems" in the Bible have never read it! They simply repeat what they hear from teachers, professors or friends. Start with one of the Gospels–Matthew, Mark, Luke or John–and see what they say. God still speaks, and He speaks through Scripture.

Second, there's the witness of the Spirit. In Romans 8:14-17, Paul refers to an incredible truth: the fact that the Spirit "witnesses" to us that we are children of God. No one knows quite how this happens, but you will find that there are times when a "still small voice" inside your heart will speak. Often that's the voice of the Spirit of God. He provides answers to questions. He offers comfort in trouble. He makes prayer feel like a real conversation with a Father. God lives inside us. He will provide that inner witness to assure us we are really His.

Third, seek out friends and fellow Christians who can provide godly advice and counsel on a problem. Go to someone you trust and pour out your feelings. Often, just verbalizing them to another human being helps greatly (pick a human, though dogs aren't bad, and I've known some very insightful cats, too).

In the last century, G. Campbell Morgan, before becoming a famous preacher, struggled with great doubts about the Bible. At that time many theories were flung abroad about the Bible and where it came from. Many said it wasn't written by the people it says it was written by. And they all said it was full of errors.

Morgan felt perplexed and fearful. Nonetheless, he took action. Gathering up all those books he'd been reading about the Bible, he stored them in a cupboard. He said afterward, "I can hear the click of that lock now." He then walked down to a local bookstore and bought a new Bible, saying, "I am no longer sure that this is what my father claims it to be–the Word of God–but of this I am sure, if it be the Word of God, and I come to it with an unprejudiced and open mind, it will bring assurance to my soul of itself."[1]

Ultimately, Christianity is not a religion of beliefs on the back burner. Rather, it's a relationship with God through Jesus. God speaks and will speak to you–through His Word, through your heart, through others. Wait. Listen. Be open. He will calm the storm in your soul if you'll give Him the chance.

THE EXTRA MILE

Here are some passages that speak of the Spirit's witness and God's promise to those who need assurance:

Jeremiah 33:3
Romans 8:14-17
Isaiah 41:10

Weekend:

What if I Don't Believe?

It's always possible. For each of us there comes a point of decision.

I remember well the night I became a Christian. A friend named Dusty Cross and I smoked some marijuana together. We ended up in my parents' basement talking and listening to music. Nine months before, I had read Hal Lindsey's book *The Late Great Planet Earth* and was so scared by what Lindsey had written that I was praying and reading my Bible in earnest. Rank terror is probably the best way to get people like me back to God! Now that I had graduated from college, I wanted to make it big. Only problem was I had no idea what to make it big in. All the spaces seemed to be filled!

That night, though, Dusty and I talked about life and its meaning–always a good subject for people high on drugs when they're most likely not to make any sense whatsoever! Dusty also seemed to be going nowhere, and I felt a desire to "straighten him out." It was a classic case of the blind leading the catatonic.

Eventually, we hit on the subject of ultimate problems like death and God. The drug had worn off and our discussion became more comprehensible. At one point, I asked him, "Do you believe in Jesus Christ or God?"

He answered, "I don't know. I've never thought about it that much."

And then he did something I'd never had happen to me before. He asked me the same question.

Before I read Lindsey's book, I'd probably have said no. Or shoved aside the question with a flippant, "Oh, who knows the answer to that one?"

But for some reason I couldn't swat the question away with a joke. For a few fleeting moments I pondered the issue. Deep down I felt I couldn't just sluff it off. I finally said, "I don't know why, but I believe that Jesus Christ was the Son of God."

Dusty had no further comments and we began talking about other subjects. But from that point on, strange things began happening inside me. Little more than 24 hours later I felt as if I knew God personally. As Friend, Leader, Guide and Helper, as well as other things. He had become real to me.

Today, I think about that moment in that smoky, drug-laced basement room. What if I had thrown it off? What if I had not "confessed" my belief in Christ? I don't know the answer to that one. But I suspect God might legitimately have said, "All right, go your own way."

I might have gone on to live a normal and even happy life–without Christ.

For each of us there comes a moment of final decision. You have to make your choice: will you follow or not? If you say no, you could live a happy, decent, even good life. But one day you will stand before God and answer for everything. I for one would not want to face that moment without Jesus at my side.

THE EXTRA MILE

Here are a few texts that speak of what happens to those who reject Christ:

John 8:23-24
Matthew 7:21-23
Revelation 20:11-15

Monday:

Making the Connection

How does anyone become a Christian? How do you personally make the connection with Jesus so that your sins are forgiven and you inherit eternal life?

There is only one way: believe in Him with all your heart, soul, mind and might. When the Philippian jailer wanted to know what to do to be saved, Paul answered, "Believe in the Lord Jesus, and you will be saved" (Acts 16:31).

Recognize you're lost, confess your sins and say to Jesus in prayer, "Lord, I trust you for my forgiveness and salvation and everything else. Please take charge of my life."

There are hundreds of ways to take that step. Many pamphlets and tracts provide insight about this. From the "Four Spiritual Laws" to one I like called, "How to Have a Happy and Meaningful Life," the process is laid out. But if you look at the conversions in Scripture, you see several common threads. First, a person recognized his sin and his need of forgiveness and salvation. Second, he learned about Jesus and all that He had done. Third, he expressed his desire to know and follow Jesus. Fourth, he obeyed Christ by being baptized and uniting himself with other believers.

Paul gave the Romans a succinct but complete statement of how to be saved: "If you confess with your mouth, 'Jesus is Lord,' and believe in your heart that God raised him from the dead, you will be saved" (Romans 10:9).

Confess Jesus as Lord.

Believe in your heart that God raised Him from the dead.

It couldn't be much simpler. Why isn't it more complicated?

Why should it be? God has made it so that virtually anyone anywhere can take that step, from a child up to the most intellectual adult.

God can't make it easier for you. Confess. Believe. Repent. Trust. They're all bound up in it. All you need is to do it.

THE EXTRA MILE

Read these passages that speak of people who trusted Christ in different situations:

Acts 2:37-42
Acts 9:1-19
Acts 16:13-15

Tuesday:

How Do I Know It Took?

"But I don't feel any different."

"Nothing seemed to happen to me."

"How do I know I did it right? Everything feels the same!"

People experience new faith in Christ in many ways. Some folks go through an emotional transformation. They weep over their sins, or they talk about being "filled with joy." Sometimes they even do strange things like speak in tongues or stand up and praise God as if possessed.

For every believer there is a different experience. God does not cut out Christians like cookies. He doesn't stamp each hand so that it shows up under an ultraviolet light when you walk in the door.

So whatever experience you have or don't have matters very little in the long run. Initial experiences and passing feelings won't hold a person in the faith, and the lack of them won't drive a person out. If you truly believe, you will believe whether the day is hot or cold.

Still, we need to be sure. "Am I really in?" a friend once asked me, as if he had joined a club.

It all comes down to belief in what God says and time. First John 5:13 says, "I write these things to you who believe in the name of the Son of God so that you may know that you have eternal life." John wrote to a group of believers who weren't sure about their salvation. Some doubted. They wanted to know their sins were forgiven, they had eternal life, and they were "in" the kingdom of God. So John gave them an answer: "I write these things to you who believe in the name of the Son of God so that you may know that you have eternal life."

Do you believe? Does something inside your heart answer, "Yes! Yes! I really do believe in Jesus"?

Then John says you may *know.* Not hope for. Not imagine. Not wish. No, he says that you may *know* you have eternal life.

If you believe in Jesus as your Savior from sin and Lord of the universe, you have eternal life. It's that simple. If it doesn't seem real yet, give it time. Talk to the Lord. Ask Him to help you see you're His. He will answer, for He says, "My sheep listen to my voice" (John 10:27a).

THE EXTRA MILE

Review more passages on this subject:

John 5:24
John 3:16-18
John 20:30-31

Wednesday:

What If I Mess Up?

Martin Luther, the great religious reformer of the 1500s who initiated the Great Reformation, pointed out one of the devil's most powerful deceptions. Satan loves to tell a new Christian he's lost God's love or support because he committed a sin, or several sins. "Take his name out of the book of life, Gabriel. He didn't put the cap back on the toothpaste tube!"

Too many of us get this idea that because we're Christians we have to be perfect. The truth is that none of us ever stops sinning, even though we hope as Christians we will sin less and less.

Martin Luther himself often battled this point with the devil. He tells how the devil came to him one day with a long list of sins: "Martin, your tongue is too quick to condemn. You were mean to the children today. Your temper is out of control," etc. When the devil was finished, Luther said, "Think a little harder, you must have forgotten some."

So the devil dredged up a few more goodies.

Then Luther drew his sword. "That's fine, but you did miss some. Regardless, I will write across the whole list in red ink this eternal statement: 'The blood of Jesus Christ His Son cleanses us from all sin' [1 John 1:7b]."

The devil left immediately. He could say nothing to such truth.

Remember, Satan will tempt you and tell you the most horrid things. He seems to have the power to speak into our minds at times. Beware of letting him get to you. Most of all, remember that the same Jesus who forgave you everything at the point of salvation continues to forgive you now. He never stops forgiving, so long as you come to Him in faith and repentance.

Are you afraid you've messed up? Stop the thoughts going round and round in your mind. Halt it all and write over it: "If we confess our sins, he is faithful and just and will forgive us our sins and purify us from all unrighteousness" (1 John 1:9). When God forgives, He doesn't just forgive the things we happened to confess. No, He forgives those sins we've forgotten about, too, and everything else in between.

THE EXTRA MILE

Consider these verses and maybe even memorize one or two for handy use when those evil thoughts come into your mind:

1 John 1:9
1 Peter 2:24
Matthew 28:20

Thursday:

What Does He Want Me to Do?

If you're convinced you're a believer now, and I hope you've taken that step, then there are other aspects of Christian living you will want to take part in. One of the most important is obedience. That can be a bad word in some circles. Obedience smacks of that "sword on the neck, do this or I do you" mentality that some have.

That is not the brand of obedience God desires. Obedience in God's eyes might better be called freedom–freedom to do what's right, to be good and kind, to gladly and joyfully choose not to tell a lie when you're in a tight spot, to earn honest money instead of resorting to illegal or ungodly means.

Real obedience is not always easy, nor does it always bring about the results we might hope for. But it always pleases God. Above all, it encourages us. When we obey, we feel good. Just like following Dad's instructions can make you feel happy and even fulfilled for that moment, so it is with God. When we obey Him, we're truly happy in ways we could never be without that obedience.

There are several ways you can obey Christ as a new Christian:

First, get baptized. This is a controversial issue among Christians. What should you do? Read up on it. Learn what your own church says about it. Think and pray about it. Study the Scriptures that talk about baptism (look up the words "baptize" and "baptism" in a concordance–a book that lists the location of different words in the Bible). Then do what you feel God would have you do. Baptism is an act of obedience to God's Word.

Second, get involved in a church that teaches the Bible. More on that later.

Third, find some fellowship with your peers. A youth group is best, perhaps one that meets during the week for fun, Bible study and encouragement.

You might ask, "Why are you being so vague about these things?" Because they're all issues you have to work through for yourself. God has given you freedom–and a brain. Use both of them wisely and cautiously, but once you've decided upon a course of action, stick to it until the Spirit shows you otherwise.

THE EXTRA MILE

Here are several texts speaking to the above issues:

Matthew 28:18-20
Hebrews 10:24-25
Acts 2:42-43

Friday:

Can I Fall Away?

Almost every Christian faces this problem sometime: Can I lose my salvation? Could I ever do something that would make God say, "Cut him off and send him to hell!"?

This also is a difficult subject in Christian circles. There are those who say, "Once saved, always saved." There are others who claim, "It's like shaking hands. If you pull away, you've lost it."

Several verses guide us into the truth in this area. Jesus said in John 10:27-29, "My sheep listen to my voice; I know them, and they follow me. I give them eternal life, and they shall never perish; no one can snatch them out of my hand. My Father, who has given them to me, is greater than all; no one can snatch them out of my Father's hand."

Look at several things here:

First, Jesus says His sheep "listen to" His voice. That's what happened to you when you became a Christian. You "listened to" His voice. Jesus sought you out. He wanted you from the very beginning. He searched for you and worked with you till you came to believe. He never would have given up till you listened because He wanted you to be one of His.

Now don't get mixed up on issues like predestination and election and so on, if you know what they are. The point is that your salvation is not something you did on your own, but something He worked in you. If He was involved from the start, you can be sure He'll take it all the way to the end. In fact, that's what Paul said in Philippians 1:6: "He who began a good work in you will carry it on to completion until the day of Christ Jesus." Your salvation is not just up to you. Jesus was involved from the beginning.

Second, notice it says, "No one can snatch them out of my hand." That's pretty plain. No one in heaven or on earth can steal you away from Christ.

Try memorizing Romans 8:38-39 about this. It says, "For I am convinced that neither death nor life, neither angels nor demons, neither the present nor the future, nor any powers, neither height nor depth, nor anything else in all creation, will be able to separate us from the love of God that is in Christ Jesus our Lord." In other words, nothing anywhere can separate you from God.

Still, some will say, "But what if I decide to leave? What if I decide to separate myself from God?"

That could be possible if you'll answer me one thing. Do you think you could ever want such a thing? Not if you've become a true Christian! My experience is that knowing Jesus is so fantastic, I could never want to leave Him. If I did, I'd suspect I never had the real thing to begin with.

God is far greater than we can imagine. If He can do all things the Bible says, then surely He can keep each of us who truly believe from losing the very thing His Son died to make possible.

THE EXTRA MILE

Review these passages and think about them in relation to your security in Christ:

John 10:27-30
Romans 8:28-39
Jude 24-25

Weekend:

Is Jesus My Lord?

There is one more thing about Christian living you should know about before we continue: the Lordship of Christ. Can a Christian accept Christ as Savior but not as Lord? Or, put another way, can you just take the good part of salvation–forgiveness and eternal life–without taking the tough part–obedience, worship, love and discipleship?

The answer to that one isn't easy. At this very minute, several recent books take opposite stands on the issue and all of them were written by people whom I personally respect and admire.

One thing must be clear at the start: you can't divide up Jesus into Lord and Savior. He is Lord, Savior, Master, King, Friend, Advocate and numerous other things all the time at every moment, regardless of how we happen to be trusting Him at that same moment.

Another thing: few of us understand all the responsibilities of Christian living when we first become Christians. All of us will go through a lifelong precess of growth that will bring about changes in outlook, few of which we can predict or even avoid. There have been times in my life as a Christian where I was rankly disobedient, not caring what God said about anything. Fortunately, I have always, after a little while, repented of those times and come back to a true walk with Him. But anyone who caught me in one of those "bad" periods might be tempted to say, "You haven't accepted Jesus as Lord."

Finally, most everyone knows so-called Christians who have "accepted Christ" but never seem to change, grow or become committed to Him in any way. Some people say they're "baby Christians" or "carnal Christians"–controlled by sinful desires–and that they have not accepted Christ as Lord. They're exhorted to repent and "rededicate their lives to Christ," things like that.

Again, this is not an issue we will ever resolve theologically. But maybe there's a solution that you can live with for right now. Christ calls us to believe in Him. That's a heart, soul, mind and might kind of thing. It's total commitment of life and breath to Jesus as our personal Discipler and Leader. It's possible a person might not realize all those things about Jesus for weeks, months or years after his conversion. But I personally don't see how anyone can say they're a believer in Christ and then go and live a life that contradicts everything Jesus teaches for months, let alone years. It doesn't make sense, just as a girl who says she loves some guy but never thinks about him or talks to him could really love that guy. It's not what we think of as love.

Thus, if you're wondering about this issue, relax. Jesus is Lord. He wants you to follow Him.

He also wants to fill your life with every spiritual blessing. Keep that in mind and all will be well.

THE EXTRA MILE

Read these texts and comment on what they say about Christ's Lordship over our lives:

1 John 2:4-6
1 John 3:2-3
1 John 3:9
1 John 4:20-21

Chapter 2

We're All in This
Together

Monday:

The Need for Fellowship

I sat alone in the bus terminal, fuming. I had gotten a ride from college to home, but on the way I discovered the car had drugs in it. I knew I had to get out. So I did. Then, after getting dropped off in the middle of nowhere, I turned around, stuck out my thumb, and the first person that came along was a policeman.

He stopped and told me to hop in. "I'm going to give you a ticket and take you to the bus station.

Hitchhiking is illegal. Don't you know that?"

"Yes."

"Why did you get out of that car between towns anyway? Was there a problem?"

I didn't want to get my friends in trouble. I said, "Difference of opinion. It didn't work out."

"Yeah, I understand."

The officer seemed friendly enough. We talked about the dangers of hitchhiking, then sports. I told him I had recently become a Christian and explained how it had changed my life. He listened with interest, but said little. When we reached the bus station, he suddenly said, "I've decided not to give you the ticket. But get a bus, okay?"

I nodded. "I will. Thanks."

I walked inside and found out I'd have to wait two hours till the bus to Philadelphia arrived. The fare was twelve dollars; I didn't have much money, and my earlier ride would have only cost me five. I felt cheated. Why did God have to let these things happen?

I waited impatiently, feeling angrier and angrier. As a new Christian, I had this idea that God made all things work out. This definitely was far from worked out. I argued in my mind. As I sat there fighting the Spirit in my heart, three students walked in with Bibles in their hands. They began passing out tracts. They were Christians. I wasn't about to introduce myself.

But the Spirit had other ideas. "Go to them," He seemed to be saying. "Just tell them you're a Christian."

No way, my mind retorted. I'm mad.

But the Spirit finally won. I got up, stepped over, and as if I was turning myself in after a crime spree, I said, "Yeah, I'm a Christian, too."

They were instantly turned on. With excitement, they questioned me about how I became a Christian, what I was doing, etc. It went on and on. As it turned out they were students at a local Bible college. In fact, one of them said his parents would be driving down to a town near Philadelphia the next day. Would I like to stay the night, get a good meal, have some fellowship and meet a lot of turned-on Christians?

I was amazed, but I bit. And I had a great weekend.

Fellowship. Amazing word. Fellows on a ship. Thrown together at sea.

It's something every Christian needs. Regularly. It gets those spiritual juices flowing and opens the heart and mind.

THE EXTRA MILE

We all need friends who are Christians, people who will support us, encourage us, and just offer an ear and a kind word now and then. Look at several biblical kinds of fellowship:

Acts 2:41-47
Acts 4:32-37
Acts 9:26-31

Tuesday:

Cookies and Coke

What is fellowship?

Perhaps you've heard the Greek word that we translate "fellowship." It's *koinonia*. It means a number of things, but primarily "sharing association, communion." Classical Greek writers used the term when they described the marital relationship. A closeness and intimacy of concern, love, care. The word also meant "generosity" and "the willingness to share your most valuable possessions with other believers."

That's quite a far cry from the "cookies and Coke" meetings that churches often have and call "fellowship."

But in reality, cookies, Coke and *koinonia* go together. Because it's when we talk, listen and encourage that we learn to be friendly and outgoing, willing to start and build the kind of relationships that will ultimately go far beyond cookies and Coke.

Recently, some friends came over for an evening of hamburgers and hot dogs, potato salad, politics, economics and theology. We got embroiled in different discussions as we talked. Different interests surfaced. Occasionally, someone revealed a problem they were struggling with. We looked at the Bible, then listened to an old Doobie Brothers album. We laughed, told jokes, quipped a few witticisms and decided we didn't do this enough.

It's not that complicated. You don't have to invite some high-powered Christian musicians to get it going. It's just a few Christians sitting around talking about whatever they want to talk about. And touching occasionally on faith, the Lord and the one thing that draws them together: commitment to Christ.

Fellowship happens when two or three gather in Christ's name.

Fellowship starts when a believer reaches out and touches another. Fellowship builds up those who are partaking of it, just as food and drink give the body fuel and music can soothe the soul. There have been countless times that I have spent a day at work feeling miserable, alone, depressed and deeply tired. Then I go out to a church fellowship and suddenly feel energized, empowered, electrified.

We thrive on it and die without it.

A young man in Burma said as he was leaving his fellowship group one night, "I came here a flickering torch, but I go a flaming torch."

It doesn't always happen that way. But it can if you dip into it body and soul.

THE EXTRA MILE
Look at these moments of fellowship in Scripture:

Acts 16:25
Acts 18:1-4
Acts 20:36-38

Wednesday:

Where Should I Fellowship?

You'll have to decide early on where you'll meet with other Christians, build relationships and disciple others or be discipled. Obviously, the first place to look is your home church. If you grew up in a church and became a Christian at an early age, there is good reason to make that your church home.

But often, people who become Christians in their teens find that their home church does not "click" with them the way they'd like. Perhaps the church does not preach or teach the Bible as God's Word. Or maybe it's so small that you don't have any friends there. Maybe your parents don't even go. You became a Christian because a friend invited you to his or her youth group.

This is not time to get radical. If Mom and Dad want you to continue in your home church, respect their wishes. You may be able to work out a compromise, though, by offering to attend the main services at that church but also get fellowship at the other church that features the dynamite youth group. Talk it out. Listen to your parents and speak your heart. Above all, don't get nasty about it. God wants us all to honor and love our parents no matter what church we attend. The important thing is work with your parents, respect their opinions, and remember that God can and will help them to direct you.

If you're a new Christian and all these bubbly feelings are simply flooding through you, beware. A spiritual high often leads to a deadly spiritual down. The rule is: stop, think, pray and look before you leap into another fellowship or church or anything else.

The most important element of church life is the preaching and teaching of the Word of God. If you're not getting such instruction, you will soon find yourself adrift with no real anchor to control those surging feelings.

In a word, try these steps:

1. Don't make any changes on the spur of the moment.
2. Listen to your parents, friends and others. Get good, biblical counsel.
3. Be confident that God loves you and will lead you as you call on Him.

Remember Hebrews 13:5b: "Never will I leave you; never will I forsake you." That's a powerful promise. Trust it and allow it to color your outlook.

THE EXTRA MILE

Here are several passages to study when considering a change of church or fellowship:

> James 4:6-7
> Matthew 18:19-20
> Psalm 27:14

Thursday:

Impressing Others

A pastor visited a family from his church and at one point he wanted to quote from the Bible. He asked if they would get him theirs. Dad turned to his daughter, age six, and said, "Honey, would you go get our Bible for the pastor?"

The daughter gave her dad a quizzical look and he added, "You know, that big thick book we look at all the time."

A few minutes later the daughter returned and triumphantly handed the pastor the latest Sears catalog.

Ever notice how Mom and Dad act a little different on Sundays and around the pastor and other Christians? The family can be driving to church and having an argument the whole way about the new earring in John's left ear and how he's not wearing it into church and so on and so forth. And what is John thinking? "What a bunch of hypocrites!"

How do you look at your parents' very real and very apparent weaknesses? You know the truth on them and sometimes can't square that–especially if they are very committed Christians–with what you know is right. You may be high on the new youth group and all you're learning and maybe Mom and Dad are even glad about this new change in your life, but maybe you also notice that Mom is moody and Dad has a wicked tongue. Or that Mom tells little lies now and then to cover up, and Dad has been known to drink more than he should. You may find this hard to accept.

Moreover, you might get to know people in church who act one way there and another way in other circumstances. You'll think it's hypocritical and false and may even suspect they're not really Christians at all.

It's possible they haven't truly accepted Christ; it's also possible you need to give them some slack. We're all sinners on the bus called earth. We all make mistakes. We all have habits that we hope won't get printed in the paper or passed from you to others by means of the gossip hotline.

Romans 15:7a points the way: "Accept one another." That's so important in the church. It's easy to criticize and put people down and think they're uncool or nerdy or duds. But remember, they could be doing the same thing to you.

What's church all about? It means accepting one another and loving one another despite our sins and occasional bad behavior. It's not easy to do. What's easy is to sit back and smirk and think how superior you are. But that's a great danger, because pride has a way of ending up flat in the dirt.

Remember, no one in the church is perfect. That includes you and me. Give me a break, and I'll try to give you an even bigger one.

THE EXTRA MILE

How should we treat one another in the church? Read these passages:

Romans 15:7
John 13:35
Romans 12:9-21

Friday:

Don't Get Much Out of the Sermon

A professor of mine tells a story about preaching in a mental institution. About three minutes into his message, one of the inmates stood up and said, "This is the most boring speech I ever heard."

This ruffled my prof a bit, but the inmate sat down so the prof continued on. A few minutes later, the inmate was back on his feet. "This is definitely the most boring speech I have ever heard anywhere, anytime."

Again, my prof winced, but he couldn't quit in the middle like that. He kept pouring out the gems. Finally the inmate stood a third time. "This is far and away the most boring speech that has ever been given in history."

This time my prof was mortified. He almost stopped right there. But no preacher ever stopped in the middle of a sermon no matter how dull and uninspiring, so he finished. At the end, one of the doctors walked up to him and extended a hand, saying, "I hope you weren't discouraged by what that inmate said during your speech."

"Well, actually, just a little," the prof said.

"Well, don't be," said the doctor. "Because we're very encouraged. This is the first time that man has ever made any sense!"

I like the story and often use it at the beginning of my own spellbinding messages. Why? Because getting up week after week and stoking interest in people for twenty or thirty or forty minutes on subjects many of them already know a lot about is tough. Unless you've been a pastor, you have no idea what terror it can be to watch people losing consciousness as you speak. Jokes like, "I go to St. Anesthesia" and "Our pastor goes down deeper, stays down longer and comes up drier than anyone I know in underwater work!" don't help.

What do you do when the sermon just isn't interesting? Just what the rest of us do: be quiet, try to be attentive, find something to think about (from the message, not Betty Lou in the next pew over) and pray for your pastor to get better. He's learning, too.

From another standpoint, our world is so over-stimulated that almost every pastor has an impossible job come Sunday. We all regularly see movies honed to hold us tight and teary for two hours. We can turn on any prime time TV show and find potent entertainment for thirty minutes without a yawn in sight. It's easy to look at preaching the same way.

Nonetheless, teaching the Word of God is not entertainment, even though some preachers can be very entertaining. So how do you get the most out of a sermon? Try these on for size:

1. Look for a kernel of truth in the sermon and turn it over in your mind. Think about it. You don't have to pay attention to every word to get something out of the message.
2. Have a Bible handy and read the passage he's talking about. Read before and after and ask the Lord to open your mind to something in the passage.
3. Come into church in an attitude of prayer. Ask God to speak through your pastor.

Above all, remember, your pastor is human, and he undoubtedly struggles with every sermon, both in the study and during the preaching.

So pray for him, love him and when you can, encourage him with an honest compliment.

THE EXTRA MILE

Look at several responses in Scripture to people's sermons and consider how that relates to you:

Acts 7:54-60
Acts 20:7-12
Acts 26:24-29

Weekend:

The One Anothers

What is church about? Is it all worship services, preaching and teaching?

To look at many churches today, you would get that impression. The majority of people who participate in church come to the main services and that's all. Some churches feature Sunday school and church on Sunday morning, then an evening service, and finally a midweek service of prayer and Bible study. That pattern seems to be fading out as more churches try to get all the meetings done on Sunday morning. But is that all church is–the main services?

Scripture says far more about how members of the church should treat one another than it does about services and teaching. In fact, the Bible says more about personal conduct toward others than anything else!

The Bible's a big book, though, and difficult. Where do we start? The "one another" concepts offer a good one. Scripture tells us a number of things we are do for and be for "one another."

Paul calls us "members one of another" in Romans 12:5 (KJV). That speaks of our connectedness. We can't act as if other members of the church don't exist!

In Romans 12:10, Paul says, "Be devoted to one another." That's a toughie. Devoted? That's real concern, care and compassion.

The same passage says to "honor one another." To honor means to show great respect and reverence.

In Romans 15:7, Paul tells us to "accept one another," which we talked about earlier. That is unconditional acceptance, even if they're a bit nerdy or dorky!

In Romans 15:14 (KJV) we find this phrase: "admonish one another." That means to point out unruly or wrong behavior when it arises. We can't ignore a brother or sister's ill treatment.

Again, in Romans 16:16, Paul says, "Greet one another with a holy kiss." Yo! I can think of lots of girls I might want to greet that way! But Paul is speaking of welcome, plain old being glad to see each other.

In Galatians 5:13 we find the expression, "serve one another." And in Galatians 6:2 (KJV) the words, "Bear ye one another's burdens." Similar ideas. In other words, be ready always to lend a hand and to help.

Ephesians 4:2 tells us to "be patient, bearing with one another," even when some of our number may be obnoxious or socially backward.

Ephesians 5:21 says, "Submit to one another," which means to literally "put yourself under" the authority of others when it's called for.

Finally, we find in First Thessalonians 5:11, "encourage one another." Everyone needs encouragement and we should be liberal in laying it on.

All these passages show how important our treatment of the saints is to God. So how are you doing?

THE EXTRA MILE

Why not look at three or four of the texts listed above and come up with practical ways you can live them out in your youth group?

Monday:

The Lone Coal

A man once came to Dwight Moody, a famous evangelist, and protested that he did not think going to church and being a member of a congregation was necessary for every Christian. The man said he could go it alone and didn't need church at all.

Mr. Moody and his friend stood near a fireplace with a roaring fire. Moody picked up a pair of tongs, and drew a bright coal out of the fire. Then he set it on the sill of the fireplace. There its light promptly began to fade and eventually the coal died.

The man smiled at Mr. Moody and nodded. "I'll be there this Sunday."

You might find yourself asking, "Why do I have to go to church? It's not that interesting and . . ." You may come up with many reasons you feel fellowship is unimportant. But like that lone coal which died without other coals around it, spiritual life fades and dies without fellowship. This is especially true of the early years of a Christian's walk with Christ. We need the encouragement, friendship, support and plain old *nearness* of other Christians. Peter said that Satan "prowls around like a roaring lion, looking for someone to devour" (1 Peter 5:8). That's absolutely true. You may not see the enemy, but he is there, tempting, deceiving, lying and goading you into sin as often as he can.

To this day, over twenty years since I came to know Jesus, I find the need of fellowship crucial. I have one group that I attend every other Friday. It's a pitch-in dinner–we all bring casseroles, fried chicken, salads and desserts, and we eat, talk, laugh and then have a speaker give a message. Afterwards, we break into groups to discuss the message. We try to apply the principles to our lives. Finally, we have dessert. There have been times when by Friday I'm so wiped out that I don't want to see anyone. Recently, I hesitated about attending the meeting, when suddenly I said to myself, "But what will I eat?!" That got me in gear.

Break bread with other Christians regularly. Share meals and conversation over a hearty piece of Kentucky Fried. It's good for us just to laugh, share our burdens and pray. Having those kindred spirits "pulling" for us is power beyond this world. And it can defeat Satan every time.

THE EXTRA MILE

Read these passages and think over what they reveal about the need for fellowship with other Christians:

1 Peter 5:6-9
Philippians 1:12-15
1 Thessalonians 3:5-8

Tuesday:

Speaking the Truth in Love

My father and I sat down in the plush Sir Walter Raleigh Restaurant and engaged in small talk before ordering our meals. I knew something was up. He had requested this meeting. Recently, my uncle–Dad's brother–had died. I spoke at the funeral, but I had gone a little too far in some of my comments. I knew I had, but I thought it had all blown over.

Something else had happened, too. Because of problems between my wife and my family, we left after the funeral without saying goodbye, or even offering condolences to my aunt. I was ashamed of my behavior. I should have given that last word even if my wife objected.

Dad and I ate and talked, and then as we both finished our meals, Dad launched into his talk. He spoke gently but forcefully. He related how my speech at the funeral had started well, but then got off on a wrong tangent. Some of the things I said were really out of line and not my place. I agreed and apologized.

Then he mentioned the other matter. I started to make a defense, but he said, "Mark, you have to get this thing under control. I know you love Valerie and are trying to do the right thing, but you wronged your aunt and all of us by simply leaving. Whatever complaints Valerie has don't warrant this kind of treatment."

I humbly swallowed my defense. There was none. I had been wrong. Finally, I said, "I'm sorry, Dad. I'm trying to work these things out."

He smiled and then expressed his support and love for me. "You are my son, Mark, and I only want what is best for you and your family. I love you, and I wouldn't be telling you this if I didn't."

I knew he was sincere and I choked back a few tears.

What had my dad done? He had spoken the truth in love. It's a powerful means of helping an erring Christian see his mistake. Paul gives the command in two places in Ephesians 4: "Instead, speaking the truth in love, we will in all things grow up into him who is the Head, that is, Christ" (4:15) and "speak truthfully to his neighbor, for we are all members of one body" (4:25b).

It's one of the most powerful teachings of Scripture and a primary way to lead others to change when they need to. Notice the two sides of the coin:

Speak the truth–that's laying it all out in plain language.

In love–that's your attitude, one of kindness and gentleness, persuasiveness that is also flexible and willing to listen.

Undoubtedly there are things that bother you about family members or church friends. Perhaps there are things you know are downright wrong. What can you do about it? Ignore it? Fume privately, but act like all is well otherwise? Gossip about it to others?

No! Speak the truth–in love. It often gets the results you want and seals a friendship with trust and respect.

THE EXTRA MILE

Read Ephesians 4:15 and 25; think of ways in which you might use this principle this week.

Wednesday:

Encouraging One Another

I felt acutely nervous. A pastor friend invited me to speak to his congregation during a month of meetings for instruction and fellowship. He specifically wanted me to use the chapters from my first book as the point of takeoff. That night, I chose to tell the story of Esther.

None of that, though, was why I was nervous. The real reason was that my dad would be there. He hadn't heard me speak in several years. The only previous time he'd had a few rather barbed comments about my style. I knew he was trying to help, but deep down I wanted to blow him away this time with a message so profound and fascinating, he would have to compliment me.

The group gathered. I launched into my story. And soon everything was flowing. It was dramatic. At several points, people laughed uproariously. I felt really good. At the end, I knew I'd done an exceptional job. Thus it was when Dad said nothing afterwards, I felt deeply chagrined. But I decided that even if he didn't like it, I'd done my best.

The next day Dad called me into his office. (I was working in the same company as him at the time). After I sat down, my heart thrumming, he said, "I want to tell you that your message last night was truly exceptional. Interesting–I didn't even look at my watch once. And it had depth. We really learned something. I was impressed."

His words floored me. Dad had never been so lavish in his compliments before. I figured, though, that this was all leading to a big let-down. I awaited the criticisms. But he just said, "That's it. It was an excellent job, Mark. I give you an A-plus."

Now my jaw was hanging. But you know what? That little experience happened over seven years ago, and I still turn it over in my mind now and then.

Mark Twain said, "I can live a month on a good compliment." Someone else put it this way: "Encouragement is the oxygen of the soul."

God wants us to encourage one another. Paul wrote, "Therefore encourage one another and build each other up, just as in fact you are doing" (1 Thessalonians 5:11).

Just as that word from my dad encouraged me, so you will be encouraged as others compliment or exhort you about something you have done well. The words will nourish you in the deepest parts of your soul.

And in the same way, encourage others. Compliment them. Exhort them to keep on keeping on. Send a note of appreciation. Give thanks. There are so many ways to do it. But the important thing is to get out there and encourage!

THE EXTRA MILE

Read how Jesus and others encouraged in these passages:

Luke 22:31-34
John 14:1-3
2 Timothy 1:3-12

Thursday:

Being There

In 1976, I suffered from such serious suicidal depression that I finally admitted myself to a hospital for it. I was a student at seminary at the time and very worried that I would not graduate if things continued.

As I spent my days in the unit, talking about depression and trying to find a way out of it, a number of friends visited me. Nearly every afternoon and night people came by to offer encouragement, prayer and a listening ear.

One of the other patients, a very attractive girl named Marla who was best known for dressing in black leather, watched one day during a visit from some friends. She said later, "You must have the biggest family on earth!"

I didn't know what she meant. She said, "All these visitors. No one has as many visitors as you. Who are they?"

I explained about seminary and church and my neighborhood. She was amazed. "I've never given much attention to church," she said, "but this has turned my head, that's for sure."

I call it "being there." Christians often think they must find some "incredible word from God" when they visit friends who are hurting. Or they suppose they need "just the right verse" that will meet the concern of the hour.

But I have found that listening, counseling, playing a game or sipping Cokes can be a powerful tonic to those who suffer. James said, "Religion that God our Father accepts as pure and faultless is this: to look after orphans and widows in their distress and to keep oneself from being polluted by the world" (James 1:27).

Pure religion is . . . visiting orphans and widows?!

Absolutely. And the sick. And those who are discouraged or depressed. Jesus tells us in Matthew 25 that one day failure to visit the sick, help those in prison, clothe the naked and feed the hungry will be reason for judgment! And heaven will welcome those who did do such things as heroes and heroines!

You have a contribution to make. Even if it's just a batch of cookies for a shut-in or sending a card to the sick, it all goes a long way. God will honor you for every little deed of compassion, kindness and love.

THE EXTRA MILE
Read and think about these passages:

Matthew 25:31-46
James 2:14-26

Friday:

Hanging in There

Ever go rock climbing? Yo! Now that is tough. Scaling a cliff, even if there are plenty of hand-holds, rocks my soul in the bosom of Abraham. Fortunately, I have always gone rock climbing with people who know how to do it. They would tie us in on a belaying line and then as we climbed, some very alert (I mean *extremely* alert) person at the top reined in the line so that if you slipped and fell, you fell only a few feet.

The last time I went was years ago, but some-times I get shivers just picturing the scene in my head. On one climb, I remember coming up against a jutting of rock where I had to hang out over dead air for a moment to get around it.

"Keep on going!" someone yelled.

"Hang in there, you'll make it," another person

was saying.

And, "Don't give up. Be patient and work at it."

In a way I didn't want to hear that. I just wanted to get around this pimple—no, this carbuncle of rock that was blocking my path. I huffed with exhaustion as I searched for a handhold. I didn't want to fall. After all, I was the youth pastor. We had courses on this in seminary.

In desperation, I lunged to get a fingerhold only inches out of reach.

And that was it! I fell—a few feet—then dangled from the belaying line like a rag doll.

"Take a rest and try it again," a leader told me. I decided that was what I needed. I eventually did conquer that rock, but it took several tries.

I bring this up because many things in life, including fellowship in the church, are like rock climbing. You suffer falls, mistakes and blowouts that put you on the sidelines. Then at other moments you're king of the hill, coming over the edge of the cliff like Spiderman and raising your arms in triumph.

Mostly, though, it takes sheer gritty nerve to keep on going.

What do you do then? Hang in there. Keep on keeping on. Refuse to give up. Paul said it this way, "Forgetting what is behind and straining toward what is ahead, I press on toward the goal to win the prize for which God has called me heavenward in Christ Jesus" (Philippians 3:13-14).

Press on. The Christian life is a race, a long distance run, a climb up a cliff. So don't give up.

Even when you fall, get up again and keep on going. One day you will face Jesus Himself and He will say, "Well done, good and faithful servant!" (Matthew 25:21a).

THE EXTRA MILE

Look at Philippians 3:1-16 as a primary passage about the need to press on despite setbacks in the Christian life.

Weekend:

Your Leaders

It was Paul's last journey around the Roman world. He burned to visit with one of the first churches he'd ever planted, in Ephesus. He realized this might be his last chance to encourage the believers. So as his ship sailed into Ephesus, he sent out word to the elders, "Come."

They came, and Paul launched into a speech. He reminded them of their first meeting and how he'd labored among them, not shrinking from telling them the whole truth of the gospel. He told them that bonds and prison awaited him in Jerusalem where he was going. They were grieved and pained.

Then he told them not to grieve. He was not so important that he shouldn't suffer. Rather, he only wanted to finish the course that God had laid out for him.

And then he told them something that shook those elders to the depths of their souls. "I know that after I leave," he said, "savage wolves will come in among you and will not spare the flock" (Acts 20:29). He warned them over and over that perilous days lay ahead. They should be watchful, on the lookout, always sober and ready to do battle.

When Paul finished, they prayed together and then embraced, hugging and kissing one another as they wept. Paul had been the means Christ used to save each of those Ephesians. And now they would never see him again!

It's a painful scene, but also a reminder of the love that God's people have for their leaders. As a member of a church, remember your leaders–your pastor and his associates and assistants. Pray for them. Encourage them. Let them help you, and when you can, offer to help them. They have a high task from God–the nurture and growth of your life in Christ. In fact, the writer to the Hebrews said, "Obey your leaders and submit to their authority. They keep watch over you as men who must give an account" (Hebrews 13:17a).

"Those who will give an account!" One day men and women will stand before Christ and will be required to tell what they did to help and guide you in the faith. That's all the more reason for you to cooperate and love them.

What can you do to help the leaders in your

church? Here are several things:

1. Love them. Don't gossip behind their backs or put them down.
2. Encourage them. Be honest about your compliments and anything you wish to tell them to build them up.
3. Serve. Do one job and do it well. Only take on other jobs if you can do them equally as well.
4. Pray for them. Always. As often as you think of it.
5. Befriend them. Be friends, ready and willing to help.

Healthy leaders mean a healthy flock. And a healthy flock means a healthy you.

THE EXTRA MILE

Read First Thessalonians 5:12-14. How does this passage say we are to treat our leaders?

CHAPTER 3

Life's Most Powerful Resource

Monday:

What Is Prayer?

Prayer is talking to God. Conversing. Saying something to Him and then listening for His still small voice. Taking a text of Scripture and asking the Spirit of God questions, then waiting for Him to answer through other resources.

Prayer speaks of all kinds of conversation we have with God. It involves confession of sin, praise, thanks, intercession for others, petition for yourself, argument, disagreement. Anything you can talk about to God–which includes every-thing–comes under the heading of prayer.

Dwight Eisenhower, who commanded the Al-lied forces in Europe during World War II and who later became president of the United States, was a man of faith. He said, "Personal prayer, it seems to me, is one of the simple necessities of life, as basic to the individual as sunshine, food and water–and at times, of course, more so. By prayer I believe we mean an effort to get in touch with the Infinite."

Getting in touch. Reaching out. Extending a hand and then locking on.

Prayer is difficult. There is no activity that demands greater concentration than praying for more than a few minutes. It's easy to repeat the same prayer over and over. But that really isn't prayer. Jesus told His disciples not to use "vain repetitions" (Matthew 6:7, KJV) in their prayers because many words repeated over and over didn't get God's attention any better than a few words uttered thoughtlessly.

No, real prayer calls for concentration, effort, energy. That's what makes it especially hard.

How do you learn to come to God that way? Someone once said, "Ask with a beggar's humility, seek with a servant's carefulness, and knock with the confidence of a friend."

Look at those three ideas:

First, a beggar's humility. You have a need. There is something you want. So you come as a beggar, a needy person who cannot get the thing for himself.

Second, there's the servant's carefulness. A servant is commanded to do something, and he goes about it carefully and wisely. When we come to God, we need that outlook. We can't ask frivolously. We ask about those things we really do need and want and believe He would grant.

Third, the confidence of a friend. Above all, God is a friend. We need to see Him as Someone most willing to do what we ask.

Pray with those traits in mind. In fact, ask Him to make those characteristics part of your life. Above all, pray–as long and as frequently as you can.

THE EXTRA MILE

Read Matthew 6:5-15 for Jesus' thoughts on prayer. What principles does He consider most important as we learn to pray effectively?

Tuesday:

A-C-T-S

If you've gotten up some morning resolved to pray for fifteen minutes or so and two minutes into the prayer time you've run out of things to talk about, take heart! It happens to the best of us. George Whitefield and John Wesley, two of the great evangelists of the 18th century, often disputed about their differing views on God. Whitefield was a Calvinist who believed that everything that happens in life happens because God made it happen. Wesley was an Arminian who took a more man-centered viewpoint. He believed that people were responsible to take action and not assume that God would just make things happen.

One night, the two friends were staying at someone's house overnight, and at bedtime, Mr. Whitefield made a brief prayer and then hopped into bed. Mr. Wesley was astounded and said, "Is this where your Calvinism leads you, Mr. Whitefield?"

Whitefield just smiled and rolled over. A little while later he awoke and found Wesley by his bed on his knees. Dead asleep. Whitefield awakened Wesley and cried, "Mr. Wesley, is this where your Arminianism leads you?"

Even the greats of faith had difficulty keeping alert in prayer.

How can anyone pray broadly and effectively? Here are some guidelines. The "ACTS" method provides some stout help. Each of the letters refers to a part of the prayer time. They are:

> A = Adoration
> C = Confession
> T = Thanksgiving
> S = Supplication

First, **adoration**. You adore God with praise for His person, character, deeds and word. Take Psalm 150, or 23, or 8 and simply use the words as a guide for adoring and praising God. This part will get your prayer time off on the right footing. It will set your mind in the groove, recognizing God as great, good, wise and perfect.

Next, **confession**. Think through the previous day and confess any sins you committed. Evil words or thoughts. Harsh arguments. A lie. Being nasty with someone. Not following though on a job. Ask the Holy Spirit to bring to mind anything you need to confess. Then confess it and get it straight with God. If it's necessary to apologize to someone, or make restitution, do so. It's crucial that we keep our conscience clear of guilt and regret.

After that, **thank** God for recent answers to prayer, the good things that happened in your life that last day, and any victories that came along.

Last, make **supplications**. Pray. Make your requests known to God. Sometimes using a list is wise. That way you won't forget anything. At the same time, bring the requests and needs of others to God–family, friends, missionaries, people at church, in school, at work, the government, and so on.

Using A-C-T-S can be a real spark plug to your spiritual life. It's not the only way to pray–but it's a start.

THE EXTRA MILE

Look at two prayers of Paul's and see how they fit into the A-C-T-S idea.

Colossians 1:9-12
Philippians 1:9-11

Wednesday:

Making Requests

A pastor told his two sons one night about a missionary in far off Sri Lanka. He mentioned many of the dangers she would face and that one of the greatest problems there was the poisonous snakes. Little Freddie, age five, took his words seriously. The night at bedtime, he prayed, "Oh, dear God, please take care of Miss Price. Keep her safe from those snakes."

The family learned later that Miss Price had been returning one night from a meeting when she encountered one of those snakes. It raised its head back, ready to attack. Then, without a cue, the snake turned and fled. Miss Price thanked God for deliverance. Later, she received a letter from the pastor. He wrote, "Little Fred never forgets to pray for you. Two Sundays ago he asked the Lord most earnestly to keep you from being harmed by the snakes." Miss Price backtracked and found the snake had fled the same day Freddie prayed.

Coincidence? Perhaps. But the truth is that God answers prayer and responds to our requests, however trivial we might think they are.

When you begin making requests to God in prayer, remember several things:

First, be specific. Don't just pray for "Africa" or "school" or "work." Pray that the family in Africa would get the house they need, or that you'd be able to prepare well for the test in school the next day.

Second, be fervent. Impress on God how important this answer is. Show Him why He should answer with a yes. Lay out your argument. Don't just mention it as if you could care less!

Third, be vigilant. Expect that God will answer. Be on the lookout. If you've made a certain request, why not follow it up with a line in your prayer notebook that describes the answer?

I used to keep a prayer "file" of requests on three-by-five cards. I'd put one request on each card and then take a whole pack at a time and pray "through" them. Whenever I saw some specific answer to a prayer, I'd write it down and file it in my "answers" file.

Recently, I went through some old files and found literally thousands of cards on which I had written God's specific answers. Not many of them were miraculous or even extraordinary. But the fact that so many had a specific answer amazed me. I found myself giving thanks all over again.

THE EXTRA MILE

Study through Nehemiah's prayer in Nehemiah 1:4-11. What elements of prayer do you see mentioned here? In what ways does Nehemiah provide a guideline for true fervent and determined prayer?

Thursday:

Praise and Worship

For many people the idea of praising God seems a tad egotistical. Does God really need all this praise? He enjoys it, certainly. It strengthens our relationship, of course. But ultimately, praise is the natural response of a loving heart. Don't you praise those whom you love and respect? Don't you talk about them with reverence, put them on a pedestal, and "rave" about them now and then?

Praise is just that. It's telling God you appreciate Him and love Him. It's laying out the reasons that you enjoy Him and value His friendship. You might compliment a friend on a job he did. Some will shout out their approval to a baseball player who smacks a hit with two outs in the ninth. Or a boyfriend might tell his girlfriend all the ways he loves her. Praise of God is the same kind of thing.

Start with the Psalms. They were meant to be

read and shouted and proclaimed with or-
chestral accompaniment. Use them as a point of
departure. Reading some out loud in your room
can be a turn on. Try it.

What should you praise God about? Several
things:

His person–who He is: Creator, Lord, Master,
Savior, Friend.

His character–what He is like: righteous, gentle,
holy, omnipotent.

His works–in history, in the Bible, in your life.

Get a little heated up, too. Emotion in prayer is
rarely a bad thing, unless it's public and insin-
cere. Dr. Leslie Weatherhead, who has written
many books on the spiritual life, said, "What is
wrong with emotion? If Christianity is falling in
love with Christ, has anyone ever fallen in love
without emotion? Can we imagine somebody ad-
vising a young lover saying: 'I would not marry
her if I were you, you evidently feel too deeply
about it.' How could anyone come into contact
with the living Christ and feel both His forgiving
love and His relentless challenge without the
very deepest emotion?"[2]

So get down and get excited. If you want to
shout it out, do so. If you feel more comfortable
alone in your bedroom, being very sincere and
very quiet, God is just as pleased. Praising God is
honoring Him as number one in your life. So let
Him know He is.

THE EXTRA MILE

Read Psalm 145, a psalm of praise, and see the many ways the psalmist finds to extol and honor God.

Friday:

Making Your Case

Rocky Bleier played running back in the 60s and 70s for the champion Pittsburgh Steelers. During his rookie season, Rocky went to Vietnam at the height of the war. He came back nine months later, a casualty. His right foot was a half shoe size smaller than his left, and the instep of that foot had been shredded by a grenade during a firefight. Two toes were badly damaged. Shrapnel had pulverized his right leg from foot to thigh.

When the grenade exploded at his feet, Rocky was thrown behind a clump of bushes. He had no weapon, he was alone, cut off from his squad, and he could hear the enemy talking and moving about. It was then that Rocky Bleier prayed a very direct and blunt prayer. He said, "Dear Lord, get me out of here if You can. I'm not going to [fool] You. I'd like to say that if You get me out of here alive and okay, I'll dedicate my life to You and become a priest. I can't do that because I know that's not what I'll do. I don't want to promise anything now and then change

my mind later when things are going good. . . .
What I will do is this. I'll give You my life . . . to
do with whatever You will. . . . I'm not going to
complain if things go wrong. If things go good, I'll
share my success with everybody around me.
Whatever You want to do, wherever You want
to direct me, that's fine. This is the best I can
do."[3]

Bleier survived and went back to playing ball
for the Steelers. He became a stellar halfback,
turning into one of the most effective blockers
the team had ever had. And he testified frequently to his experience behind those lonely
bushes in Vietnam.

That prayer illustrates how to make a case with
God. Sometimes I think of prayer as akin to a
lawyer making his case in court. You present your
argument. You show the jury why they should go
your way. You deal with the objections. And then
you rest and leave it in the jury's hands.

That's real prayer. When you present to God
not only what you want but why He should
answer with a yes, you are praying wisely and
effectively.

I always liked the story of the pastor's son who
got caught in a severe thunderstorm and ran all
the way home. Lightning and thunder crackled
overhead. It was a perilous night. His father happened to see him the last thirty yards and
noticed as he ran his lips were moving. As the
boy careened into the house, his dad said, "What
were you saying as you ran, Son?"

The boy shuddered. "I was reminding God that I'm the son of a minister."

I think God must have liked that prayer, too.

THE EXTRA MILE

Read Psalm 13. How does the psalmist make his case before God? How can you use the same principle in giving God your requests?

Weekend:

Using Scripture as a Guide

"When you pray, you must always pray according to God's will, or He will not answer with a yes."

How many times have you heard something like that in a sermon? It's important to pray according to God's will. Whatever we ask of God must be acceptable to Him. No, not just acceptable. It must be something He already wants to do for us.

So how do we know what things God already wants to do? We're not mind readers. God's up there in heaven and we're down here. How does anyone know what God wants for any of us?

It's easy–read the Bible. Most of what's in there is what He wants for you, me and everyone else. Take any of the epistles of Paul and you will immediately discover a hundred things that are absolutely God's will! It's right there in black and white.

If you want to pray according to God's will, simply turn Scripture into prayer. For instance, a favorite passage of mine is First Thessalonians 5:16-18. It says, "Be joyful always; pray continually; give thanks in all circumstances, for this is God's will for you in Christ Jesus." Why not turn that passage into prayer? "Lord, teach me to be joyful always. Just like Paul says. To be joyful wherever I am, whatever I'm doing. Next, help me to learn to pray continually. And give me an attitude of gratitude (for the poetry buffs in the group). Teach me to do these things–consistently, joyfully, reverently."

How hard is that? The Bible becomes our source book for knowing God's will on every subject!

Of course, this says nothing about all those daily, specific mundane problems that aren't in Scripture: the test on Tuesday; getting that job you applied for; the hockey game on Saturday night; whether Julie will go out with you or not. None of those things are in Scripture and so you can never be sure if they're "God's will" in the classic sense.

But that's another thing that Scripture speaks to. In Psalm 37:4 you'll find a verse well worth memorizing and using. "Delight yourself in the LORD, and he will give you the desires of your heart."

Look at that! What a promise! God will give us

whatever we desire. All we have to do is delight in Him.

Now turn it around. If you delight in God, what will happen? The more you love the Lord, the better you will understand His plans for you. How does anyone know what another person wants or desires? By getting close to them and spending time in their presence, asking questions, talking, walking together, thinking about them. When you delight in the Lord, your desires come into line with His. Then you begin to want what God wants truly!

God's will is not difficult to discover when you open the Scriptures with a delighting heart.

THE EXTRA MILE

Memorize Psalm 37:4 and pray about it. Discuss the passage with the Lord and come up with several ways you can delight in Him today.

Monday:

Continual Prayer

One of the befuddling commands of Scripture is found in First Thessalonians 5:17. There Paul says, "Pray continually." Paul was a valiant defender of the faith, the foremost apostle, a marvelous missionary, and undoubtedly a potent pray-er. But a pray-er who never stopped–twenty-four hours a day?! That doesn't make sense.

Exactly. The problem is solved when we look back at the original Greek in which Paul wrote. When he said, "Pray continually," he used a word that means "without reaching a permanent end point." The same word was used of a hacking or recurring cough. We are to pray in a repeated or recurring fashion. In other words, we never sign off permanently.

How does this happen? Like any other kind of relationship, prayer goes on and off as things occur to the pray-er. Imagine for a moment that Jesus Christ is physically present with you wherever you happen to be. Think of Him as a friend who goes where you go and walks where you walk.

You head off to the store. Jesus is right there with you in the car. You need to do some homework. Jesus is sitting there on your bed watching. You hit the high school football game. Picture Jesus right there with you in the stands, roaring along with the crowd.

With Him ever present like that, what's likely to happen? Well, every now and then you make a comment to Him. "What did you think of that?" Or, "This problem is really getting me. You have any ideas?" Or, "I think I'll ask Darcy out tonight. Think she'll go?"

You see what happens. You talk to Him be-cause He's there–literally. Sometimes you may feel like shouting, "This is great, Lord. God is so good, you know what I mean?" At times, you thank Him for a sunset or a perfect rose or a really hilarious joke. You pray all the time because He's there with you wherever you are. You can't ignore Him. How could you, and still be on friendly terms? So you naturally include Him in everything you do.

That's continual prayer. You praise Him, give thanks, confess a sin, offer a request, or intercede for others. It's all mixed up. You aren't following an outline like we did in the A-C-T-S sequence. You just let whatever comes into your mind work its way onto your lips.

Why pray like this? Because that's how any relationship works. You talk, you listen. You give, you take. You muse, you argue, you discuss. Whatever happens to be in your mind at the moment is legitimate grist for the prayer mill.

THE EXTRA MILE

Ask the Lord to make you aware of His presence and to respond to that presence in continual prayer. Why not make that idea a request for prayer itself?

Tuesday:

The Lord's Prayer as a Help

"The Lord's Prayer" is an important tool for prayer and worship. Jesus told His disciples how to pray and gave them this little formula:

> Our Father who art in heaven, Hallowed be thy name. Thy kingdom come. Thy will be done in earth, as it is in heaven. Give us this day our daily bread. And forgive us our debts, as we forgive our debtors. And lead us not into temptation, but deliver us from evil: For thine is the kingdom, and the power, and the glory for ever. Amen. (Matthew 6:9b-13, KJV)

Many people repeat this prayer word-for-word each Sunday and at other times. Until prayer became Madelyn Murray O'Hair's target in the 60s, that prayer was part of the morning exercises of every public school in the United States. We sat at our desks and prayed this prayer each morning right after the Pledge of Allegiance.

Jesus didn't give that prayer as something to repeat over and over, though, even in one sitting. Rather, He meant it as a model prayer that includes all the basic elements of prayer in a few words. There's praise and adoration: "Our Father who art in heaven, Hallowed be Thy name."

We get in line with God and His plan and pray according to His will: "Thy kingdom come. Thy will be done in earth, as it is in heaven."

We petition Him and make a personal request out of need: "Give us this day our daily bread."

Next, we confess sin: "And forgive us our debts as we forgive our debtors."

Again, we request that God "lead us not into temptation, but deliver us from evil."

And finally we wrap up with the words, "For thine is the kingdom, and the power, and the glory forever. Amen."

This was Jesus' model for all prayers. In fact, this prayer can become an outline for your prayer time. Start with the exact words of the prayer, "Our Father, who art in heaven . . ." And then begin ad-libbing your own variations: "O Lord, you are great and majestic. I praise You for coming into my life and changing me day by day. It is so good to know You're with me . . ."

You can see it offers a great outline to use in your quiet times with God. So why not try it next time you pray? And let the Spirit lead you as you come up with your own thoughts, praises and specific requests.

THE EXTRA MILE

Read over the Lord's Prayer in Matthew 6:9-13. If you already know it, try using it as a guide for your next prayer time and share with a friend how it worked.

Wednesday:

Where Are All the Answers?

Peter Marshall led prayer as Chaplain of the

Senate in the 1940s in Washington, D.C. He said, "I know that [God] is far more willing to do things for us than we are to ask Him. And that is the great mystery. Knowing what I do about God's power and God's willingness to help, I keep on struggling with myself and trying to work things out in my own way when He could save me all the anxiety and do it better and easier. I believe God is made sad at the sight of so many of us trying to work things out for ourselves. He longs to help us, but we won't let Him; we won't ask Him."

To be sure, there are some folks who resort to prayer only when everything else has failed. We don't think of asking God to get involved until we're flat on our backs and beaten.

On the other hand, there are times when we do pray, honestly seeking God to guide us through some troublesome situation. And then nothing happens. It looks like God hasn't answered at all. Some prayers go unanswered for months, if not years. George Mueller, one of the great prayer makers of history who raised over seven million dollars to help orphan children in England in the 1800s, prayed for a friend's salvation for eighty years! Mueller died before that prayer was answered. Nevertheless, after his death, his friend actually became a Christian.

Many of us pray for the salvation of a loved one, healing of an ailment, solving of a bad job situation or finding a life's mate to no avail. God seems to do nothing. In fact, sometimes the situation can get worse. That can go on for years, even decades.

Why doesn't God answer some prayers that seem so legitimate? Scripture spells out a number of reasons. Sometimes we pray selfishly and that gets no answer (James 4:1-3). At other times, we are simply not praying according to God's will (1 John 5:14-15). If we are hiding some sin in our life, God will not even hear our prayers according to Psalm 66:18.

But there are many times when God delays or doesn't seem to answer. It raises severe doubts in our minds. Some say that God answers three ways: "Yes," "No" and "Maybe" (or "Wait"). Sometimes we see an immediate answer. The other day, my three-year-old daughter hid my alarm clock. It was late at night and I wasn't about to awaken her. So I simply prayed. Less than a minute later, as I looked around, an idea popped into my head to look in a not-so-obvious place. There it was. God answered my need immediately.

On the other hand, I have prayed about some things that I later realized were not what I really needed. In some cases, I've even been glad God didn't answer, because I might have ended up in severe trouble over it. For instance, I often prayed in dating relationships that "she would be the one." Many "ones" didn't work out, and thank God for that!

Most often, though, prayers get a "Maybe." Or,

"You'll just have to wait." Why? Maybe conditions aren't right for an immediate answer. Maybe God has to make other things happen before He can work out this request. Or maybe in God's wisdom, the delay is good because it will give us time to change.

Don't lose heart. God doesn't overlook any prayers we offer Him. He answers them all–sometimes long after we've forgotten we even prayed them.

THE EXTRA MILE

Read Acts 12:3-17 for an interesting example of a place where God answered a prayer and the Christians didn't really believe He could answer that quickly.

Thursday:

The Prayer Journal

David Livingstone (1813-1873) traveled over 30,000 miles on foot evangelizing Africans in unexplored territory. He used to keep a diary. Every year on his birthday, he would write a prayer. His last birthday alive on earth he wrote. "O Divine One, I have not loved Thee earnestly, deeply, sincerely enough. Grant, I pray Thee, that before this year is ended I may have finished my task."

One night later that year his coworkers found him on his knees by his bed, dead. He had died praying and his prayer of months before had been answered.[4]

While our goal may not be to die on our knees, Livingstone's keeping of a journal offers a useful example. A journal provides not only a way to record what you're praying about, but also a means to keep a record of answers. You can also write down in it any thoughts or insights you gain from those prayers as well. Livingstone's own journals give us a rich source of personal stories showing a man living by faith on the cutting edge of adventure.

If you decide you'd like to try keeping a journal, what should you include in it? Here are several ideas:

- Specially crafted prayers
- Specific requests, and the answers to those requests
- Lists of the needs of others
- Thoughts and insights gleaned from time spent studying
- Quotes and favorite verses of Scripture you might want to memorize
- Anecdotes and stories you hear from other Christians, in church, in the workplace, in the home
- Wrestling with doubt, questions you have for God

- Passages you've studied and principles gained

Undoubtedly, you will include much more in your own private journal. As I looked back through the journals I kept years ago, I found it was very encouraging, much like reviewing an old picture album. Thoughts I had "way back when" startled me. I can see a pattern of growth. When I've gone through rough times, my journal chronicles the changes and transformations that occurred over a period of time. In this respect, a journal can be a tremendous help. You can use it as a diagnostic manual when you go through troubled periods. It will rebuild faith when you've had serious doubts and worries.

Don't feel you must write a journal entry every day. Be flexible about it. In fact, beware of putting yourself under any strict discipline that is manmade. It can become a form of legalism that induces great guilt when you fail–and for no reason. There's nothing in Scripture that says we must keep a journal and write in it every day.

Use it as a help to growth. And if it ceases to interest you, don't hesitate to try other methods that you find more useful.

THE EXTRA MILE

Try keeping a record of your prayers for one week. See how many were answered. Write them down in a journal. Why not share several of those answers with a friend?

Friday:

The Prayer Cycle

Dick Eastman's book *No Easy Road* illustrates beautifully the power of sustained prayer. He quotes a man named Oscar Schisgall on the fruit of a regular prayer time: "If you devote but one hour a day to an engrossing project, you will give it 365 hours a year, or the equivalent of more than forty-five full working days of eight hours each. This is like adding one and one-half months of productive living to every year of life."[5]

The idea of praying for an hour every day daunts most of us. Not many know how to fill up one hour of talk with God, let alone one hour every day. But if you're organized, it's not difficult. That is why I developed a tool I use that I call my "prayer cycle."

On the extra leaves of my pocket Bible, I have written five lists of "cyclical" things, people, organizations, and whatnot that I pray about. For instance, in cycle one, I divide the prayer list into a chart of five days with different categories of prayer for each day. During that week, I pray for:

- My family–listed by name with specific needs and requests that I know about

- Missionaries–by name and with specific known needs (two listed per day)
- Families in my neighborhood–two listed per day
- Publishing houses I work with (this is only for writers!)
- Groups I know about–like Concerned Women for America, The Rutherford Institute and Campus Crusade for Christ
- Magazines I write for

During the second week, I use this list:

- Continents–Africa, Asia, etc. with anything specific going on that's been in the news
- Nations in the world–I pray about anything I've read in the news that relates to a country, too.
- Churches I know of or have been associated with–two per day
- Leaders in the church worldwide–people like Billy Graham, radio preachers, etc.
- States in the U.S.–three per day with any specifics in the news
- Pastors I know

You can add as many items as you want. Breaking up the list into many bitesize pieces makes it easier to pray consistently and regularly about numerous items. Imagine getting to heaven and learning how you personally influenced world history through your ardent praying!

You can see how easy it is to fill up an hour using such a method. One thing I do is walk while I pray. That gives me a chance to get some exercise, too. Don't feel you have to go into your bedroom or some private place. God hears as well in the mall as by your bed.

THE EXTRA MILE

Read Psalm 63. Where do you see the psalmist praying? What does this indicate to you about where and when you can pray?

Weekend:

Plodding Along Day by Day

A young, single man from San Francisco moved into a woodsy area. One night, a lone raccoon poked its nose up at his window and he gladly went out and fed it. The next night, the raccoon returned with her brood, a bunch of hungry, eager mouths. The bachelor happily fed them, too. He got into the habit of doing this, until one night arriving home late, he discovered he'd run out of the dog food he gave to his woodsy "pets." He told the group sitting restlessly in his back yard, "Sorry, guys. Nothing here for you tonight."

He went back into the house and thought that was the end of it. But in less than five minutes there were ringed eyes and black noses at every door and window, scratching, tapping and making an awful racket. Raccoons climbed onto the roof and stamped their paws. One thrust a hairy arm through the vent in the bathroom!

Thinking they'd give up in a few minutes, the man bided his time. But after an hour of this racket, he gave up. He got out of bed and, having nothing else to feed them, he made stacks of pancakes for the whole army of hungry raccoons.

One of my favorite passages of Scripture is Luke 18:1. Luke speaks of how "Jesus told his disciples a parable to show them that they should always pray and not give up." Jesus then gave them the parable of the unjust judge. A woman who wanted legal protection went to the judge and made her request. The judge refused. But she came so often and implored him so fervently that he finally granted her request. He was afraid she'd wear him out. Jesus contrasted this man to the attitude of God. He is not unjust or unwilling to hear us, and He also respects our perseverance.

If you want something from God, something ultimately only He can provide, and you're sure it's not a selfish thing, and you believe it could well be His will, then enduring in prayer must become your plan of attack. Like those raccoons in San Francisco, and like the woman in the parable, God wants us to learn to "pray and not to lose heart." As we continue to bring our requests to His throne room, He promises that He will speedily answer.

William Carey (1761-1834), missionary to India and a translator of the Bible into several Indian languages, used to pray, "God, make me a plodder." By just taking the steps he needed each day, this man ended up covering many miles for the kingdom of God during his lifetime.

That's the person who endures: the plodder– the one who just keeps on going. Like the Olympic marathoner, real prayer calls for a steady gait, a sharply honed mind and an eager, determined gaze.

THE EXTRA MILE

Look at Jesus' parable in Luke 18:1-8. What principles do you think Jesus is getting at? How can you apply them in your prayer life?

Chapter 4

You and the Bible

Monday:

Why Is the Bible Important?

Who am I? Why am I here? Who is God? Can He be known? What happens when you die? Was Jesus real? How did the world get here? Why are things so messed up in the world? How can we straighten it all out?

Most of us ask these questions sometime in our lives, often while we're young. Some find answers; many don't. Many go through life confused, insecure, unsure of anything, worried about death and the idea of judgment, terrified that their lives may add up to nothing. As Henry

David Thoreau said, "Most men lead lives of quiet desperation."

The world can be a desperate, lonely place.

But there is a place to find answers to the questions above. Direct, complete and satisfying answers to all such questions can be found in the Bible. It is the only book that provides such plain counsel on the burning issues of life. Anyone who honestly confronts Scripture will find that its powerful wisdom speaks to the problems that tear the souls of multitudes.

Martin Luther said, "The Bible is alive, it speaks to me; it has feet, it runs after me; it has hands, it lays hold on me."

Christian Karl Bunsen wrote, "The Bible is the only cement of nations, and the only cement that can bind religious hearts together."

Timothy Dwight, one of the early presidents of Harvard University, had this thought: "The Bible is a window in this prison-world, through which we may look into eternity."

Billy Graham said, "The Bible is the constitution of Christianity."

Watchman Nee, respected author, put it this way: "Since God's Word is living, he who listens and does not live has not heard the Word of God."

The Bible itself says that it is light (Psalm 119:105), life (Hebrews 4:12), sharp (Hebrews 4:12), the breath of God (2 Timothy 3:16), pure (Psalm 12:6), living and abiding (1 Peter 1:23), faithful (Titus 1:9), truth itself (John 17:17), powerful to give faith (Romans 10:8), eternal life itself

(John 6:68), powerful (1 Corinthians 1:18), sanctifying (1 Timothy 4:5), and "useful for teaching, rebuking, correcting and training in righteousness" (2 Timothy 3:16b).

If we have a question touching on the meaning or direction of life, chances are the Bible has a plain spoken answer.

THE EXTRA MILE
Look at several Scriptures in which the Bible talks about itself:

2 Timothy 3:16-17
Psalm 119: 9, 11, 18, 105

Tuesday:

Is It Really God's Word?

From the start, we need to ask, "Is the Bible really and truly the Word of God? Or is it just another book among many?"

I like the story of the youngster who came home from Sunday school and told his dad, "The pastor told us a wonderful story about how the Jews were thrown out of Egypt and then chased by the army of Pharaoh. When they saw the roaring chariots of the bloodthirsty soldiers, the Jews built a bridge over the Red Sea and walked over it. Then when the Egyptians tried to follow, the Jews put dynamite under the bridge. When all the chariots were on the bridge, the Jews blew it up and all the Egyptians ended up dead at the bottom of the sea."

"Is *that* the way the pastor told the story?" exclaimed that boy's amazed father.

"No," the kid finally answered. "But if I told you what the pastor told us, you'd never believe it."

The Bible is full of stories, some earthy, some down to earth and some downright astounding: the ten plagues of Egypt; Jonah and the great fish; Elijah on Mt. Carmel; Jesus' healing and miracles–stilling the storm, turning water into wine, walking on water, casting demons out of demoniacs, feeding the 5,000, rising from the dead. All these events are told in the Bible with a plain, pull no punches, "these are the facts" manner. No frills. No really *weird* things (like in Buddhism, the belief that Buddha was born in a flower). But plenty of fantastic stuff.

We have to decide whether we buy it.

What then does the Bible say?

First, it says it's the revelation of God, Creator and Lord of the universe. It states this over and over throughout its pages. While it's true that other religious books say similar things (the *Koran*, the *Vedas*, the *Book of Mormon*), that neither proves nor disproves the point. But it does plainly indicate what the Bible thinks of itself. No one can go around saying it's just another book. Either it's the Word of God or a pack of lies.

Second, people constantly test the Bible

against that truth. Unbelievers attack the Bible because it makes such grandiose claims about itself. Throughout history, scholars, leaders, kings and potentates have tried to discredit that book. Nonetheless, it's still around. Most of the arguments others have waged against the Bible have been shown to be false, misinformed or rank lies. As someone said, "The Bible is an anvil that has worn out many hammers."

Third, the Bible claims to be *God's words*-not just a series of words and books from God, but the actual "breath" and "life" of God. When God gave us the Bible, He provided us a book with His own life in it. Just as we have life, so the Bible is alive, active, sharp and powerful. Those are not mere words and sentences you're reading; they are the very soul and heart of God Himself.

Remember these facts as you read Scripture, because it means the Bible will speak to you personally. It will do that in ways that no other book or human ever could. God Himself will speak to your heart through the Bible's paragraphs, stories, parables, proverbs and principles.

Read it with true fear-reverence. When God speaks, He never lets His Word go out for nothing.

THE EXTRA MILE

Read Psalm 23. Why do you think this Psalm is so beloved by Christians the world over? What is the source of its power? How does it affect you?

Wednesday:

What about All Those Problems?

You've probably heard that the Bible is "full of contradictions and mistakes." Secular college professors love to spellbind their students with such talk. They dismiss the Bible with a wave of their hand, and lo, all the students drink it up as if it were a personal word from the president.

It's true that there are "problems" in the Bible. How could Jonah have survived three days in the belly of a giant fish? How was Jesus conceived by the Holy Spirit and born of a virgin? Exactly how did Jesus walk on water? And still the storm? And send demons into two thousand pigs? And undergo transfiguration on the mountain before His disciples?

Scripture says little about how these events occurred. The writers don't offer any "scientific explanations" or "facts" to back up their assertions. They simply say, "We saw this happen. Jesus said this and then that occurred." They don't get technical.

Does that mean it can't be true or that it was made up? Well, take a problem from another realm. Do you know why from a scientific viewpoint that chocolate tastes so good? And why does dirt taste so bad–to humans? Earthworms love dirt. So do trees. But we humans don't like it nearly as much as chocolate (except for my three-year-old daughter, who has been known to wear dirt with every outfit she has). Moreover, why are some people born with deformities or mental handicaps? Why is every snowflake different? How is it that water makes plants grow? Why can't we drink salt water?

Certainly, we know of "scientific" reasons for some of these things. But that doesn't change our ability to enjoy and partake of the good things of life. Even though we don't understand many things in life–the beauty of taste, the power of sight, the ability to think–we still use them and make the most of them.

Thus, when you read the Bible and notice a problem, remember two things:

1. Problems can be solved with study, time, meditation and prayer. Just because you don't know an immediate answer to an apparent "contradiction" or "textual difficulty" does not mean there is no answer.
2. Problems are just that–problems. It doesn't mean there is no solution. Every endeavor of life faces problems, from riding a bike to designing a space vehicle. Because we haven't found a way to do something doesn't mean there is none. If God was completely comprehensible to us humans, what good would He be? We hardly understand ourselves. If we

figured out everything about Him, we wouldn't need Him anymore.

In the nineteenth century, scholars attacked the Bible as an error-filled book full of the most simplistic and foolish mistakes of fact, history and science. They laid out about eighty errors they believed could never be solved. They said people like the Hittites, mentioned in the Bible in several places, never existed. And that the city of Ur, Abraham's home city, was unknown in the ancient world. In the early twentieth century, though, archaeology really took off. Archaeologists proved every one of those eighty or so "errors" were not errors at all. In fact, some archaeologists argue today that their science has done nothing but "prove" the Bible a reliable and accurate document.

Someone once approached Mark Twain with the question, "Don't things in the Bible that you don't understand worry you?" Twain replied, "No, what worries me is all the things I do understand."

If you take the Bible seriously, you will spend plenty of time getting befuddled, confused and doubtful. At times, you may even think you've found a major error. Don't be fooled. The devil loves to hoodwink and sidetrack God's people with nonsense. Stick to what you do understand and know–and that will be plenty to chew on.

THE EXTRA MILE

Next time someone tells you the Bible is full of contradictions, ask them to name one. Then study it and see if you can find an answer to the puzzle. Meanwhile, see if you can find any "contradictions" now. What ones can you think of, and what answers might you offer to a questioner?

Thursday:

All These Versions

Go to a bookstore and you will find ten, perhaps twenty different translations of the Bible on its shelves. You will need to make a decision about which version you will use for study, memorization and reading. The version you memorize in will undoubtedly become your study, church and fellowship Bible as well.

Why are there so many versions? The New Testament was written in the international language of that period, *koine* Greek. The Old Testament was written in Hebrew, though a few books–Ezra, Esther and parts of Daniel–were written in the more common Semitic language, Aramaic. Obviously, to make it easy for each of us to understand the Word of God for ourselves, we must have it translated into our native tongue.

Statistically, there are some 5,500 languages in the world. Some part of the Bible has been translated into almost 2,000 of them. English, being the international language of our day, has a multitude of translations. Some are excellent. Some are not so good, being influenced by the theology of the translators (the Revised Standard Version, for example, was translated by more liberal scholars and some of their liberalisms intrude—as in Isaiah 7:14, the prophecy that Jesus would be born of a virgin; the word for "virgin" is rendered "young woman").

Some versions—the Living Bible and the Phillips version, for example—are not actual translations, but "paraphrases" and cannot be trusted as reliable for every word or idea. They should not be used as study Bibles.

Among the best Bibles for memorizing and studying are the New King James Version (NKJV), the New American Standard Bible (NASB), the New International Version (NIV), and the King James Version (KJV).

To help you decide which translation to use, consider these guidelines:

First, which version does your church prefer? Many churches place extra Bibles in the racks in front of each pew. This is usually the same version the pastor reads and preaches from. That doesn't mean this is the best version or a more accurate one. But it will make things easier if you use the same text as the pastor and others use when preaching and teaching from the Bible.

Second, which version do your friends, disciplers, parents and teachers use? Such people can probably give you good reasons for their choice.

Third, which version are you familiar with? Which one do you prefer? You can easily walk into a Christian bookstore and leaf through a number of versions to see how they read. Take a text you know and like–Psalm 23, John 3:16, Romans 8:28–and see how that version translates it. That will give you a quick and clear idea of what the rest of the translation will be like. If you don't respond favorably to the well-known texts, you probably won't like the rest of it either. You might also talk to your pastor or youth pastor about this. They may even have copies of several versions that you can try out. Either way, it's your decision.

Fourth, pray about it. The Spirit of God will guide you in this matter. He knows you may use this version for the rest of your life, so it's wise to get God's wisdom on the subject, too.

Finally, try one version for a while. See how you like it. Six months or a year in one translation will familiarize you with it completely. If you want to change after that, it won't be difficult.

The important thing is that you find a translation that fits you and speaks to you. That accomplished, you're well on your way to years of insightful and Spirit-led study and learning.

THE EXTRA MILE

Read John 3 in each of these versions: NIV, NASB, NKJV. Which do you prefer and why?

Friday:

Just Read

John Bunyan lived in the 1600s and became a great saint of the faith. While in prison he wrote a number of books, including the best-selling book of all time (after the Bible): *Pilgrim's Progress*. It remains a highly readable story today, and it graphically illustrates many of the great spiritual truths we all need to walk successfully with Christ.

Bunyan emphasized the need to read the Bible and pray on the basis of that reading. He wrote, "Although you may have no commentaries at hand, continue to read the Word and pray; for a little from God is better than a great deal received from man. Too many are content to listen to what comes from men's mouths, without searching and kneeling before God to know the real truth. That which we receive directly from the Lord through the study of His Word is from the 'minting house' itself. Even old truths are new if they come to us with the smell of heaven upon them."

Read your Bible carefully and thoughtfully. It's a powerful study method. You can read through the whole Bible in one year if you take only four chapters a day every day. On the way through you will unearth the great promises and principles that will encourage you in your daily walk with Christ.

As you read, try doing this:

1. Write down and memorize any verses that you particularly like or respond to. Memorize the verse itself and the "address" (the book, chapter number and verse number). Memorized verses function like anchors that will enable you to stand firm in the midst of the hurricanes that come into any committed Christian's life.

2. Spend a few minutes thinking about what you've read. Pray and ask the Lord questions. Write down any insights you get in a journal, diary or notebook so you'll remember them for future reference.

3. On occasion, try reading through a whole book–especially the epistles (letters) in the New Testament–in one sitting. Imagine being the actual recipient of those letters. How would you have felt if the letter had been addressed to you? Think of these as God's way of talking to you personally.

Years ago a professor told a class that the Bible was full of contradictions and that he never understood a word of it. When no one disputed the prof's statement, he seemed satisfied he'd made a grand proclamation until one student raised his hand and said, "Sir, the Bible is a love letter written from God to His children. If you didn't understand any of it, that just shows that you shouldn't go around reading other people's mail."

The Bible is a love letter from God to you and me. Read it that way and you will soon find yourself falling more in love with the author.

THE EXTRA MILE

Read the book of Philippians. Think of it as a love letter from God to you. In what ways do you see Him expressing affection, offering advice and giving assurance? Can you pick out one verse that spoke in a special way to you that you can memorize?

Weekend:

Memorizing Scripture

Abraham Lincoln once said, "I believe the Bible is the best gift that God has ever given to man. All the good from the Savior of the world is communicated to us through this Book. I have been driven many times to my knees by the overwhelming conviction that I had nowhere else to go."

Bible memorization has been the most profitable, useful and influential habit in my life. Many times during the day, these verses memorized long ago come to mind when I'm tossed and turned by opinions and the confusion of my own heart. When anxiety strikes over finances, school or a family problem, Philippians 4:6 reminds me, "Do not be anxious about anything, but in everything, by prayer and petition, with thanksgiving, present your requests to God."

In a confrontation between myself and my boss, Proverbs 15:1 reminded me how to respond to what I thought was an unjust criticism. The verse says, "A gentle answer turns away wrath, but a harsh word stirs up anger."

If I'm tempted to hedge on the amount of money I donate to the work of God's kingdom, Malachi 3:10 is there to speak to me: " 'Bring the whole tithe into the storehouse, that there may be food in my house. Test me in this,' says the LORD Almighty, 'and see if I will not throw open the floodgates of heaven and pour out so much blessing that you will not have room enough for it.' " Second Corinthians 9:6 also helps: "Remember this: Whoever sows sparingly will also reap sparingly, and whoever sows generously will also reap generously."

Memorization of Scripture impacts a life powerfully:

First, it hones your mind. As you learn the discipline, your thoughts become sharper, more logical, more under control and directed. You become a better thinker and speaker in the process. Frequently, young people who memorize Scripture get better grades as their ability to concentrate and to study in depth increases.

Second, you will make connections between different truths in the Bible. A verse in the Gospel of John will remind you of another truth in Proverbs or the epistles of Peter. You'll begin to think "theologically" and study more effectively.

Third, memorizing Scripture will calm you. Emotionally, you feel comforted, strengthened, assured, more secure. You will grow more mature as you develop your mind through that process.

Finally, memorizing Scripture helps keep you from sin. Psalm 119:9 says, "How can a young man keep his way pure? By living according to your word." And verse eleven adds, "I have hidden your word in my heart that I might not sin against you."

There are countless other benefits that you will discover as you work to store God's Word in your heart. So memorize those verses, get them lodged deeply in your soul, and never be without a good word in times of trouble.

THE EXTRA MILE

Read Psalm 119:1-18. What does this passage teach you about memorizing and meditating on God's Word? Do you see any encouragement here to begin doing this regularly?

Monday:

The Quiet Time

The very fact that you have a Bible is a miracle. A minister named Rev. Paul Chang fled from China as a teenager. Years later he returned carrying a precious gift: Chinese Bibles. In a few hours after he arrived he had given them all away except one. That one he saved for his 83-year-old mother.

When Chang and his mother were reunited, they held one another and wept a long time. His mother prayed aloud, "Heavenly Father, I thank You. You've answered my prayer of the last thirty years. You've brought my son back. You've preserved him. You are using him as Your servant."

Then Rev. Chang presented his mother with the last Bible he'd brought back. His mother held it to her breast and prayed again, "Father, I thank You. For the last fifteen years I have been longing for a Bible." Then she told her son, "You have given me the most precious gift of all."

She reached into her pocket and drew out a slip of tattered paper with deep dirty creases. She unfolded it gently and read one verse she had copied years before from a friend. It was all she had of God's Word. She never went anywhere without it. "Son," she said, "this has been my Bible."[6]

Billions of people the world over do not have

even one verse.

I write this as an illustration of the reverence and love that many people have for the Word of God. They treasure it. They defend it. And they read and study it.

Which brings us to the subject of the quiet time. In our culture, the "QT" has become a symbol of a close walk with Christ. Millions of Christians rise each day to pray and study before eating or showering. They regard the reading, study and meditation of God's Word as the only way to begin a new day. Martin Luther–an ardent scholar and reader himself–once said, "I have so much to do today that I will have to spend the first three hours in prayer or the devil will get the victory."

That said, having or not having a quiet time with God each day is entirely your decision. There's nothing in the Bible that says you must have one in the morning, afternoon or night. The Bible exhorts us to study it, memorize it, meditate on it and apply it to our lives. But it does not say how, when or where. That's your choice. You'll have to bring your own style and preferences to the table in working out a plan. How do you do it? Here are several ideas:

1. Include time for prayer, reading and studying. Divide up the time with a few minutes for each.
2. Plan a place and time where you can find quiet and solitude regularly. The impor-

tant element is undisturbed quiet. That's the reason it's called a "quiet time."

3. Beware of becoming legalistic about it. If you miss one, two or even several days, don't whip yourself about it. Every day is a new, fresh start.

4. Be flexible to change your plan as different needs and desires arise. Few of us are "quiet timing" the same way we did ten, five or two years ago. It's a process of growth. Let it grow.

The important thing above all is that you try it and work at making it a habit. You will never regret gaining this practice.

THE EXTRA MILE

Look at these verse and consider what they say about the need to study and grow in God's Word on a regular basis.

2 Timothy 2:15
1 Peter 2:2
2 Peter 3:18

Tuesday:

Intensive Study

On March 7, 1981, Colombian hit men murdered a young missionary named Chet Bitterman. Reporters and investigators hounded Chet's family in the U.S. They wanted to know if Chet had really been working for the CIA. When they learned that all Chet did in Colombia was translate the Bible into one of the tribal tongues, the reporters were perplexed. In frustration one blurted out, "But why should they kill someone just for translating the Bible? I mean, isn't that a pretty harmless thing to do?"[7]

To Americans, so used to freedom and the availability of the Bible, it's hard to understand. But the forces that killed Chet Bitterman and the powers that rage against God's Word are not mere flesh and blood. We know from Scripture that "our struggle is not against flesh and blood, but against the rulers, against the authorities, against the powers of this dark world and against the spiritual forces of evil in the heavenly realms" (Ephesians 6:12).

The devil and his forces want to keep you from reading, studying, memorizing and meditating on Scripture more than just about any other spiritual activity. Christians who attend church but do not attend to their Bibles are of little concern to the devil. But one who carries the "sword of the Spirit" and uses the Word of God deftly has a power the devil must reckon with. Let me repeat: the devil does not want you to study Scripture, get it lodged in your heart or use it in your daily life. As one father wrote in his son's gift Bible as he left for college, "This book will keep you from sin, but sin will keep you from this book."

How do you study the Bible intensively? Beware of coming at Scripture with the idea that "the Spirit will just speak" out of the verse in some mystical way. God speaks, yes. But He also told Timothy to "correctly handle" the Word by studying it diligently (2 Timothy 2:15). Real study takes thought, effort, use of study tools (Bible dictionaries and concordances, mainly), comparison of texts and reading of what others have written about the passage in commentaries.

Years ago, I learned a method of study that still works for me today. It has three steps.

Observe. Ask, "What does it say?" Read the verse or paragraph. Write down your observations of words, grammar, meanings, definitions, syntax, etc. The first assignment in seminary we received after we learned about observing was to write down twenty-five observations on Acts 1:8. Boy, did that take some effort! And then at the next class, the prof said, "Now go home and write down twenty-five more!" It was a powerful lesson. Think of yourself as a detective come to solve a crime. Look at every possible aspect. In other words, "dig" into that text as with pick, shovel and hoe.

Interpret. Ask, "What does it mean?" Find out what the statements point to. Look at the actual content of the paragraph, then the context–what went behind and what goes beyond. Compare other passages where similar ideas are discussed. Consult a commentary or Bible dictionary and see what a Bible scholar has to say about it.

Apply. Ask, "What does it have to do with me?" This is the final and essential step of all Bible study. You take it past the page and into your life. How can you use it to better your character or walk with God? Is there a sin to avoid? An attitude to change? Some faith to exercise? An example to follow? A promise to claim? An action to take? A challenge to meet?

If you approach the Bible with these three questions and goals in mind, you will find it opens up in both a practical and a supernatural way.

THE EXTRA MILE

Study a favorite passage using this method. Can you take ten minutes to write down observations, ten minutes to make an interpretation and another ten to make a few practical applications?

Wednesday:

Methods of Bible Memory (Part 1)

Bible memorization is undoubtedly the most difficult habit to get started and to maintain, but it yields life-transforming dividends once it becomes a part of your life.

In my own journey as a Bible verse memorizer, there were three different processes I used. Each enabled me to memorize thousands of verses and then whole books of the New Testament.

The first method is what I call "the Bible memory pack"—a packet of small cards with Bible verses on them. You can purchase these in stores or from a number of discipleship-oriented organizations such as the Navigators, Campus Crusade for Christ, Young Life, Campus Life and InterVarsity, but you can also easily make your own "pack." All you need is a little business card pocket folder and some blank cards. Your mom and dad may even have some old business cards in a desk somewhere that you might use for your memory pack.

Once you have the cards and the folder, write down favorite or important verses on each card. Divide them into "new" verses to memorize and "old" verses you need to review regularly. The most important element of Bible memory work is not just memorizing the verse, but reviewing it frequently enough so that you do not lose it. Start with one of the new verses and simply say it over and over until you know it. That is, repeat it this way: "John 3:16. For God so loved the world . . . John 3:16." Remember to repeat the "address" ("John 3:16" or whatever) before and after you do the verse. Once you know it, tuck that verse on the other side of the folder in the review pile. Try to get through the whole review pile at least once a day. You can review up to thirty or forty verses in less than twenty minutes of memory work a day, if you try. Learn to use "dead time" (standing in lines, waiting on appointments, before and after classes) to pull out your pack and review.

Once you've gotten the review process going regularly, you'll soon find that all those newly learned verses will fill your pack up. At that point, you might create a "Bible memory file." In this stage of the process, tape all your business cards to three-by-five cards. Then store them in a file, broken up into several categories: new verses, recent verses, weekly verses (seven dividers–Monday through Sunday), review verses, etc.; each category is separated by a tabbed card. On any given day–let's say Tuesday–you pull out three tabbed cards and the verses behind them: the new section, the everyday review section, and the Tuesday review section. I found that I could keep over 2,500 verses memorized and reviewed at least once every two months on only fifteen minutes of actual memory work a day.

I know this probably sounds rather ambitious, but it's actually very simple. And it can enable you to make some very great leaps forward as a Christian.

THE EXTRA MILE

Try memorizing these three verses. They're powerful helps to Christian living and growth.

Psalm 119:11
Romans 8:28
Philippians 1:6

Thursday:

Methods of Bible Memory (Part 2)

Using the Bible memory file is easy and accommodates almost any expansion. At the time I stopped using it several years ago, I had over twenty-five hundred different verses that I could review in only fifteen minutes of work a day. They were divided into several categories: new verses, recent verses, weekly verses (seven dividers–Monday through Sunday), and bi-monthly verses (sixty dividers so that I reviewed the verses in each section only once every two months). I found that this system kept most of those verses in tip-top memory tune. If I found that a verse or two in the bi-monthly file got out of shape–I couldn't repeat it word for word when I reviewed it–then I would simply switch it to a higher level–the weekly group, or even the "recent verses" group. I keep all the verses in a foot-long, three-by-five card file box. As I started my quiet time, I simply opened the box and took out each of the files appropriate to that day.

Nonetheless, it's probable you will eventually outgrow this system. I found I had memorized so many individual verses in some books of the New Testament that I might as well just link them all up by memorizing everything in between. This led me to the third stage of Bible Memory, the "Pocket Bible system."

For this system, I bought a pocket Bible and began working on whole books during my walk each day. (I took walks each morning to get my exercise; it was an ideal way to do my Bible memory work and meditation.) I started with Ephesians and began going through the whole Bible this way.

By way of review, I used a system similar to the file method, except I did it with whole books and chapters. For instance, once I learned Ephesians, I divided it up into six review times during the week: Monday was Ephesians 1, Tuesday was Ephesians 2, and so on.

Today, I review many of the smaller books in the New Testament on a six-week cycle. Of course, such work takes real commitment and desire. My goal for a number of years has been to memorize the whole New Testament before I vacate this body. I've still got a long way to go. But it's something that drives me.

Using such methods, you will find that your knowledge of Scripture, your ability to apply it in different situations and your panoramic understanding of the Word of God will jet into overdrive. You'll grasp the scope of Scripture. Every circumstance of life will release into your mind several words from God on the issue. Your blood will "become Bibline," as Charles Spurgeon, a great nineteenth century preacher said.

Naturally, this may all be some time down the

road for you. But remember, it's a goal to shoot for. Why not accomplish something really worthwhile?

THE EXTRA MILE

Try memorizing the Beatitudes in Matthew 5:3-12. See what knowing these truths does in your life over the next few weeks. Perhaps even write down your insights for sharing with others.

Friday:

Power, Power, Wonder-Working Power

Psalm 19 is King David's joyous recounting of the wonders of God's Word. He says that it's "perfect, reviving the soul" (19:7a). It is "trustworthy, making wise the simple" (19:7b). And its precepts are "right, giving joy to the heart" (19:8a).

He concludes, "They are more precious than gold, than much pure gold; they are sweeter than honey, than honey from the comb" (19:10).

It's hard to imagine today that God's Word is "more precious" than gold. Or, in the vernacular, money. After all, who would exchange a million dollars for a copy of a Bible? In a nation where Bibles are so available, it's inconceivable. In fact, we could even rationalize it all away: "If I had a million dollars, I'd surely give the first 10 percent to the Lord's work."

If offered a choice between a new Miata and a Bible, which would you take?

Or even a new stereo and a Bible?

Or, putting it in the lowest terms we can, a Big Mac and a Bible?

It's easy to take the jaded view above that you prefer money to God's Word. That's only because Bibles are so available today. But God has a way of putting this truth into perspective. Another text shows us the lie of the supposed value of so many other things over God's Word. Amos prophesies,

> "The days are coming," declares the
> Sovereign LORD,
> "when I will send a famine through the
> land–
> not a famine of food or a thirst for water,
> but a famine of hearing the words of
> the LORD.
> Men will stagger from sea to sea
> and wander from north to east,
> searching for the word of the LORD,
> but they will not find it.
>
> "In that day
>
> "the lovely young women and strong
> young men
> will faint because of thirst." (8:11-13)

I believe this kind of "famine" is happening in our age, at least in the United States. People have nearly everything they could need or want, but they are unhappy, fearful, angry and broken. They ruin their lives with drugs and drinking and illicit sex. They seek an answer to their emptiness in a multitude of pleasures: movies, television, exotic and plentiful foods, fast cars and the like. Yet, they don't reach any lasting satisfaction. Even the president's wife has spoken to this emptiness she sees in America. Hillary Rodham Clinton believes that we need a revolution through politics and the life of the spirit to rid us of this "malaise."

People are confused. But God's Word is there. It's open. It's alive. And it can change your life forever.

The magazine *Guideposts* wrote of a South Sea Islander who joyously displayed his Bible to a World War II GI. The soldier commented, "We've outgrown that sort of thing." The native just smiled. "It's a good thing we haven't," he said. "If it wasn't for this Book, you'd have been our meal by now."

There is power in the Word. It can transform craven cannibals into caring Christians. If you're still unsure of the need of the Bible in our country's life, try this: drive into the heart of any city at night, and get out and walk a mile. If you survive, you will not have proved that God's Word has failed. But your eyes will be opened to what happens in the world where His Word is ridiculed and forgotten.

THE EXTRA MILE

Read Psalm 19 and note the number of ways that the Word of God can have an impact on a person's life.

Weekend:

Keep on Keeping On

A new pastor wanted to find out what the students in his Sunday school knew. He walked into a class and asked one of the boys this question. "Who knocked down the walls of Jericho?"

The boy stammered, then said, "Sir, I don't know. But it wasn't me."

With genuine concern, the pastor turned to the teacher and she said, "Well, the boy is honest and I believe him when he said he didn't do it."

Appalled, the pastor stepped out of the classroom and went immediately to the superintendent's office. He recounted the story of his question and the answers he'd gotten, from one of the teachers no less. The superintendent apologized, saying, "I've had that teacher here for many years, and I am sure if she knew who knocked down the walls she would have told you."

The pastor dropped his jaw in amazement. He decided to go the chairman of the Board of

Elders about the caliber of Christians in that church. After spelling out the details of the story, the chairman finally said, "Well, after all, aren't we making a mountain out of a molehill? I suggest we just pay to fix it and enter it on the books under the heading of 'repairs.' "

Many Christians today know little about the Bible even though they have gone to church and Sunday school for years. In the last few decades we have majored on feelings and making people comfortable rather than truly giving them depth in the Word of God.

Jesus gave us a potent word in Matthew 28:19-20: "Therefore go and make disciples of all nations, baptizing them in the name of the Father and of the Son and of the Holy Spirit, and teaching them to obey everything I have commanded you. And surely I am with you always, to the very end of the age."

God wants us to make disciples and teach Jesus' truth to all. Only then can we hope to live in the kind of peace and harmony that Jesus came to bring.

How can you help out? Study, read and memorize Scripture as part of the pattern of your life.

And by the way, who did knock down the walls of Jericho?

THE EXTRA MILE

Read First Peter 2:1-3. How does a baby's craving of milk picture the way Christians should desire God's Word? In what ways do you see yourself in this passage, and in what ways would you like to see yourself?

Chapter 5

The War Within and Without

Monday:

Right Thing, Wrong Friends[8]

Quitelight and Riffleglow sat on the ledge over-looking the group of boys. They watched as one of them, Tom, pulled a *Playboy* magazine out of his backpack. They knew they weren't seen or heard, so Quitelight remarked, "You're taking notes now?"

"Of course," Riffleglow said. "That's what we recording angels do."

"Just watch Jason, then. We don't need to be

131

concerned about the others."

"All right."

Tom's strong voice rang out to the rest of the group. "Now we'll get down to business. Take a gander at this!" He flipped the magazine open to the centerfold. The moment the nude picture lay flat before them, each of the boys gave an "ahh," while Tom and two others made several cracks.

Jason sat still, hoping no one noticed he was trying desperately not to look at the picture. But when Tom looked up, Jason knew he was caught.

"What's the matter, Cartwright? Don't tell me you've gone holy on us?"

Quitelight and Riffleglow leaned forward, waiting on Jason's answer.

Jason set his jaw and flicked his blond hair out of his eyes. "It's just a picture."

"Then why don't you look at it?" Tom picked up the centerfold and held it out in front of Jason's face.

Jason couldn't help but see the picture even though he didn't want to. He tried to keep his eyes unfocused, but he felt his face flush the moment he saw it. In the same instant, he remembered how his father had spoken to him recently about sex when he turned 13. His father had emphasized, "You don't have to do anything you don't want to, Jason. Just remember that. You can please the Lord, if you choose."

It all made him feel very uncomfortable. But after an inner argument, he stood up. "I'm going back."

Tom jumped to his feet, still holding the

magazine in front of him. "What are you, a baby? A thirteen-year-old baby?" The other boys gathered around them.

"You want to be in this club, you do everything we do, Cartwright. None of this 'I'm better than you' stuff."

"I'm not better than you," Jason said quickly.

Quitelight whispered to Riffleglow. "I like his honesty."

Riffleglow nodded.

"Then what are you?" Tom said with a sneer.

Jason sucked in his breath. Quitelight leaned forward. Riffleglow wrote on the invisible pad quickly, his fingers etching the letters in golden swatches of light.

"I'm a Christian," Jason said. "That's all."

"Well, then maybe you don't belong in this club."

Jason turned to go. "Maybe I don't." He began walking away, sensing the sting of all the eyes upon his back. Tom hurled several more insults at him, but as Jason hurried through the clearing the voices disappeared. He stopped at a tree and leaned against it, biting his lip. "I'm never going to have one friend, not a single friend," he murmured. Quitelight and Riffleglow followed and watched somberly. Tears formed in Jason's eyes. He said through clenched teeth, "Why does being a Christian have to be so difficult?"

Quitelight whispered, "You did the right thing."

Jason heard nothing. But a sudden breeze cooled his face. As he turned to walk up the path toward home he muttered, "Maybe it's better to do the right thing than have the wrong friends."

Quitelight turned to Riffleglow and smiled. "There–see! Not bad for an afternoon's notes."

Riffleglow grinned. "These humans always amaze me." They both followed the boy through the woods, all the while rousing a chatter of birds and skittering a squirrel into Jason's path to give him a good laugh.

THE EXTRA MILE

Why is temptation so tempting?

Jeremiah 17:9-10
Genesis 3:1-3
Hebrews 11:24-26

Why is it important to choose friends who will emphasize the good and righteous things of life?

Proverbs 29:24
Proverbs 24:21-22
Psalm 1:1-2

Tuesday:

Testing and Tempting

Many people claim the Bible is full of contradictions. They say you can find verses that state things are one way, and then find others that picture something altogether different. One of those problems comes under the heading of temptation. Jesus told us to pray, "lead us not into temptation" (Matthew 6:13), yet He Himself "was led by the Spirit into the desert to be tempted by the devil" (Matthew 4:1).

James says that "God cannot be tempted by evil, nor does he tempt anyone" (James 1:13b). However, a few verses earlier he wrote, "Consider it pure joy, my brothers, whenever you face trials of many kinds, because you know that the testing of your faith develops perseverance" (James 1:2-3). The problem is that the same word is used in the original Greek Bible for both "tempted" and "tested." Satan tempts us. God tests us. What's the difference?

Think of it the way General Motors might come at it. For instance, say GM designs a new car in 1994 called a "Lightning." The car sports four on the floor, mag wheels and 300 cc's. It gets forty-two miles to a squirt of gas. It corners like a hockey player, accelerates like a Star Wars spaceship and stops on a dime, then gives you nine cents change. What are we to make of this modern miracle?

When GM tests that car, it tells the driver to take it through the road course "maxed out" on all curves, straightaways and stops. They want the test to show the Lightning performs the way the advertisers say it performs. The driver runs it around the course and pushes every limit till the chassis cracks. He wants to prove that this car lives up to its billing. Or else, if it does fail, he wants to expose the flaws so GM can correct them.

However, what happens when Ford arrives on the scene? They have their own ideas about what this car is made of. If anything, they'd like to show it's nothing less than a hype dream. When their expert jumps behind the wheel, he'll push that car to the limits too, but he plans to demonstrate this car can't perform. It doesn't hold the road–in fact, it's a hazard to anyone who gets into it.

Do you see the difference? God is like GM. When He put us through "tests," His purpose is to demonstrate we're really Christians. He plans that we succeed. Or else, He wants to show us our weaknesses so we can correct them. Satan, on the other hand, like Ford, "tempts" us. He longs to trip us up, knock us down and prove we're fatally flawed, worthless sinners who can't do anything right.

While God has good intentions in "testing" us, Satan's motives are nothing but evil. He plans to destroy us. But God desires to strengthen us.

You can see, then, that every test we go through has two sides: God's and Satan's. If we face them with the attitude that we will please God and defeat Satan, we can't do anything less than succeed, even if that means exposing our flaws so we can change for the better.

THE EXTRA MILE
Look at the following passages in which a per-

son was tested or tempted. What do you see that Satan was trying to do in each of these situations? What about God?

Peter in Luke 22:31-34
Job in Job 1-2
Jesus in Matthew 4:1-11
Saul in 1 Samuel 15:1-23
Eve in Genesis 3:1-7
(see also Genesis 2:16-17)

Wednesday:

Satan's Plan

In the early 70s, Don Shula became coach of the Miami Dolphins football team. The Dolphins were at the bottom of the league back then. They had one of the worst records in the history of football.

Then Shula arrived. The day he took over, he marched into the locker room and told his players that they were no longer members of a losing team. From now on they were winners. He promised that if they listened to his instructions and worked the plan he came up with, they couldn't do anything less than succeed. Each man would study his opponent till he knew that player better than his own wife. By using that plan, Shula assured them, they would begin to win.

Win they did. One year they went undefeated. They also won several Super Bowls.

To lead effectively, every leader must have a plan. Satan, our adversary, is such a leader. He has a plan. With it he wants to accomplish several goals. What is Satan's plan for your life? What are his goals when he tempts us? Let me give you five that spell out the word, "S-A-T-A-N." He wants to:

Squelch *our confidence.* When he leads us into sin, the devil destroys our confidence in God's ability to help us. The worst result of falling into sin is not the need for forgiveness; it's the belief that we're stuck, sunk and buried by our sin. He wants us to believe we'll never escape and that even God can't help us.

Attack *our witness.* The devil longs to destroy our ability to witness and serve. How many times have you heard the statement, "The church is full of hypocrites"? Part of the reason people say that is because they know Christians who have sinned in their presence. Satan uses temptation to kill our ability to witness to others.

Trigger *more sin.* The devil knows that one sin always leads to another unless confessed and repented of. When Cain sinned by bringing a faulty gift to God, God rejected it. That led to anger and finally his murder of Abel. Judas Iscariot first criticized Jesus. Soon his criticism led to rebellion and ended in complete betrayal. One sin usually leads to another, and another, and another. Satan knows that and works to make it happen in your life.

Accept *sin in others.* By giving in to sin in our own lives, we learn to tolerate other sin in our midst. Satan wants to fill the church with sin. When we feel guilt about our own sin, we're more reluctant to confront it in others. Soon, the devil turns a church into a "sin playground" where everyone tries to get away with all they can.

Not *let you gain God's riches.* Sin will keep you from gaining God's true riches. Moses knew this when he chose to leave Pharaoh's palace and join the Jews. Hebrews 11:25 says, "He chose to be mistreated along with the people of God rather than to enjoy the pleasures of sin for a short time." Satan loves to lead us to exchange God's riches of real love, joy, hope and faith for sinful pleasures like stealing, cheating, easy living and hatred of all that's good.

Satan is working his plan. It's up to us, in the power of the Spirit, to work against it.

THE EXTRA MILE

In the following verses try to determine what Satan would plan to accomplish in our lives to destroy God's will and way:

2 Timothy 1:7
Galatians 6:9-10
2 Timothy 1:8-9
James 1:2-4
James 4:6-7
1 Peter 4:8-9

Thursday:

The New Truth

Satan and his allies gathered around the fire. "Well, Boss," said one of the younger devils, "you showed the Father, you sure did."

Satan's eyes flashed. "I don't want to hear about Him. Understand? Just call Him the, the . . ."

"How about the "Big Dope?" asked one of the demons with a squint.

Satan grinned. "I like it. I like it. You deserve a promotion. What are you?"

"A Principality Sixth, Boss."

"Make it a Fifth." Satan gazed around with a wicked grin. "Whenever someone comes up with a good idea, he gets a promotion, understand?"

Everyone yelled, "Aye aye, Boss."

Then another of the younger demon disciples remarked, "So what do we do now? I mean, the Father-er, I mean, the 'Big Dope'-has all the truth on His side. What are we going to do about that? There's not much left."

Satan rubbed his chin and sighed. This was the very thing that had been troubling him for a long time. What could they do? The truth was, well, *the truth*. It was the way things were. How could you fight against that? He looked hotly around at the gathered masses. "Well?" he asked. "Who wants a promotion?"

Voices clamored all at once. Some were saying they should just wing it, others suggested they didn't have to deal with *the truth*, just get on with the rebellion, and still others remarked that it didn't matter. But Satan, being the wisest of all creatures, knew it did.

The one smaller demon with fiery golden eyes and fluttery wings said, "We invent *New Truth*, that's all."

Again, Satan rubbed his chin. A pimple was sticking up and he picked at it. "New Truth, eh?"

The demon stepped forward hesitantly, but as he spoke his voice rose with excitement. "Sure. We can say that the truth is relative, see. And we've come up with an alternative, and after all, anything is true so long as you believe it, right?"

Satan was still picking at his chin. He pushed at the pimple as he spoke. "New Truth? New Truth. I like it. I like it a lot!" Suddenly, the pimple squirted with a gush on some of the younger demons. They jumped back in disgust, but said nothing. After all, Satan was the big boss.

"*New Truth* it is," shouted Satan. "That's our plan. We will expose the *New Truth*, not the *old used up, washed up, crummy old truth*, but the *happy, interesting* and *energizing New Truth* that everyone will find absolutely fascinating."

And so, Satan and his cohorts have been using *New Truth* ever since. Only it comes out as deception, lying, accusation, temptation and testing.

After the gathering, though, two demons sat down to a cup of sulfur tea. They gazed into the darkness a long time before speaking. Finally, the older one spoke. "There's something troubling me, Maggum."

"Yes, Gribble?"

"Satan got us all to rebel on the basis of the idea that we could win, beat You-Know-Who and all. I'm wondering, is that *New Truth?*"

Gribble shuddered. "No, that's *True Truth.*"

Both demons looked into one another's eyes, then flinched away. Maggum said, "That's not what You-Know-Who says."

"The Fath-? I mean, the Big Dope?"

"Right."

"He says we'll lose."

"I know."

Gribble scratched his ear. "So what do you think of that?"

"I try not to," said Maggum wryly.

"Yeah."

They both gazed into the fire, but each wondered in his heart how much he could trust even the boss.

THE EXTRA MILE

What does the devil do according to these passages?

John 8:44
Revelation 12:10 and Zechariah 3:1
Matthew 4:1-2

1 Thessalonians 2:19
Luke 22:31-34
1 Peter 5:8

Friday:

The Power of the World

What is the world? We find the clearest statements about it in First John 2:15-16. That passage says, "Do not love the world or anything in the world. If anyone loves the world, the love of the Father is not in him. For everything in the world– the cravings of sinful man, the lust of his eyes and the boasting of what he has and does– comes not from the Father but from the world."

John isn't referring strictly to the earth when he uses the word, "world"; no, what he speaks of is a system, a whole attitude that forces God out and pretends He doesn't exist. The "world" is that mindset that says, "I'm my own person. I rule. I will make my life into something good."

Notice what is in that mindset: "The lust of the flesh, the lust of the eyes and the boastful pride of life," as the NASB says. What are these things?

The "lust of the flesh" takes our normal desire to feel good and perverts it. We all need food. But our lust turns us into gluttons. We all need sleep. But our lust tells us to sleep in (or to sleep less than we need because we have something

"big" to do). We all need friendships and relationships, but our lust incites us to satisfy that desire
in wrong ways: homosexuality, premarital sex,
adultery, and so on.

What are the sins of the flesh? Laziness, immorality, impurity, sensuality, lack of self-control,
foolish entertainments, lack of discipline, fornica-
tion, drunkenness, drugs, carousing, revelry, un-
reliability. What is the result? Complete
selfishness. The person given over to the lust of
the flesh cares about only one person–himself.

*The "lust of the eyes" takes the normal desire
to have beautiful things and perverts it.* All of us
like beautiful things. But this lust pushes us further. We "have to" have more and more and
more. King Solomon did this when he began
building programs at the expense and agony of
his people. Achan experienced this when he
stole the silver and a Babylonian robe after the
fall of Jericho in Joshua 7. Judas Iscariot gave in to
this lust when he betrayed Jesus for thirty pieces
of silver.

What are the sins associated with this kind of
attitude? Covetousness, materialism, ingratitude,
greed, hording, impatience, unkindness, unwill-
ingness to give generously to God's work,
general nastiness. When you let this lust run
your life, you end up depressed and unhappy. Ultimately, nothing satisfies you. You're like a
spoiled child.

*The "boastful pride of life" takes the normal
desire to be someone significant and perverts it.*

All of us want to matter, to think of our[...] being "important." However, this lust pe[...] the desire to be important and turns us [...] people who will do anything and hurt anyone to get ahead. King Saul had the problem. So did Cain, when he murdered Abel.

What is it that we want? Prestige, popularity, power, privileges, possessions. The sins are anger, hatred, jealousy, envy, boasting, blasphemy, disobedience, lack of forgiveness, gossip, slander, murder, contention, selfish ambition. It leads you to a state of total callousness toward others. You can't love anyone. You care only to get what you want.

An old story pictures some workers laying down a concrete sidewalk. Knowing that dogs and little children like to leave their imprint in the fresh cement, the men put up sawhorses around the section. Then they sat down under a tree to have lunch. As they ate, a very old woman with a cane passed by. She stopped at the sidewalk and took a long look. Then, to the workers' astonishment, she climbed over the barrier and wrote something with the tip of her cane. It spread out over the entire length of the concrete. When she was gone, the men jumped up and read her inscription: "Mary Beth was here!"

Ah, we all want to be somebody. But we can all take it to an extreme. Watch out. The world wants you. If you get on that merry-go-round, who knows where it'll stop?

selves as
verts
into

and think over what they
/orld:

Weekend:

The Devil's Strategy

How does the devil get us to sin?

"Easy," says one girl. "All he has to do is to get me to the mall and I'm buying."

"Right," says another. "Whenever I get into a tight spot, I'm tempted to lie. And lie I do."

The temptation of Eve in Genesis 3:1-7 is a good picture of how the devil tempts us. You may wonder about the thoughts and ideas that come into your mind. Some of them are the "thought-plants" of one of Satan's followers, a demon who has been assigned to your case for the day or week or month. He can make suggestions that occur in your mind in these ways:

To a person tempted to steal money from his mother's purse: "Why not take the money? No one will know."

To someone thinking of becoming a Christian: "Oh, you don't need to trust Christ today. Think of all the fun you'll be missing."

To a Christian going through a trial: "If that happens to me, I'll never praise God!"

What then is the process? Taking Eve as our illustration, notice this step-by-step plan.

1. *Direct your thoughts.* The first thing the devil in the guise of the serpent did was ask a question: "Did God really say, 'You must not eat from any tree in the garden'?" (Genesis 3:1b). He slithered in and directed her thoughts. He focused her on a negative and put her on the defensive.

2. *Doubt the truth.* Once he'd planted his thought and heard her answer–which was full of mistakes–he guided her to doubt the truth: "You will not surely die" (3:4a). One of Satan's best tactics is to get us to doubt God's truth. Once we doubt it, sooner or later, we'll also disobey it.

3. *Deny the consequences.* In the same breath, Satan denied what God had said: "You will *not* surely die." God had said, "You *will* surely die" (2:17b). Satan simply put a "not" in front of it, a rank obliteration of what God had said. If Satan can get us to doubt the truth, he takes us beyond doubt to total denial of the danger.

4. *Denigrate God and His motives.* Following that, Satan put down God Himself, saying that God had evil motives when He created the tree of the knowledge of good and evil. "For God

knows that when you eat of it your eyes will be opened, and you will be like God, knowing good and evil" (3:5). He was saying God held something back.

5. *Declare the wisdom of choosing sin.* Satan suggests that if Eve eats the fruit she'll "be like God." Whenever we're tempted to sin, the devil always supplies the "come-on":

"Do it and you'll get a great reward."

"Try drugs and you'll have fun."

"Drink beer, and it'll make you feel great."

6. *Draw back and let us run with it.* After planting all his sinister ideas, Satan pulls back. He lets Eve think on her own. "When the woman saw that the fruit of the tree was good for food and pleasing to the eye, and also desirable for gaining wisdom, she took some and ate it" (3:6a).

It's remarkable strategy, one the devil uses over and over in tempting us. Do you see how it happens in your own life? Are you aware of what the devil's doing? Think through the last time you were tempted. What suggestions and ideas came into your mind? Was there that seed of doubt, then the denial? Did the "voice" put down God's way and Word?

The devil isn't very creative. He employs a bread-and-butter process. Yet, it's effective. Every person on earth is beaten by it in one way or another nearly every day.

THE EXTRA MILE

Read through the temptation of Adam and Eve

in Genesis 3. Then look at these scenes and see how others were tempted:

Cain in Genesis 4:1-8
Achan in Joshua 7:20-21
Jesus in Matthew 4:1-10

Monday:

The C-A-S-E of the Foolish Christian

Whenever we use the Word of God in dealing with temptation and sin, we must learn to use it accurately and correctly. If the devil realizes we don't know what we're talking about, he'll trick us every time.

For instance, have you ever been at a party where the girls and guys have paired up? You and your date decide to take a walk. Soon you're out in the car. You know what you believe about things like sex and petting, but the girl you're with is cute, she smells wonderful, and the way she looks at you makes your heart pitter-patter almost into your throat. Then something happens in your brain.

Voice 1: "You'd better get out of the car. Things could happen you'll regret."

Voice 2: "Ah, don't worry. You're under control."

Voice 1: "But the Bible says 'flee from immorality.' "

Voice 3: "It does? Where?"

Voice 1: "Just give me a minute, I'm sure it's there."

Voice 2: "Oh, give me a break. The Bible doesn't say anything about a little kissy-huggy stuff."

Voice 3: "I'm sure it does. But where was that passage?"

Voice 1: "I'm trying to remember. It was in my devotional reading a few weeks ago . . ."

Oh yeah! The devil's got you right where he wants you. Knowing the Word–and knowing it word-perfect–is critical to success in dealing with temptation. Look at what happened to Eve. When the devil approached her in the garden in the person of the serpent, he asked, "Did God really say, 'You must not eat from any tree in the garden'?" (Genesis 3:1b). Eve answers, "We may eat fruit from the trees in the garden, but God did say, 'You must not eat fruit from the tree that is in the middle of the garden, and you must not touch it, or you will die'" (3:2b-3).

Before we go any further, we need to ask: What did God actually say? It's found in Genesis 2:16-17: "You are free to eat from any tree in the garden; but you must not eat from the tree of the knowledge of good and evil, for when you eat of it you will surely die."

How accurately did Eve understand God's word? Notice what she did–four things that spell out the word, "C-A-S-E."

She **changed** it. God said, "From the tree of the

knowledge of good and evil." But Eve changed it to say, "From the fruit of the tree that is in the middle of the garden." That's an important distinction because it means she made no attempt to understand what the "tree of the knowledge of good and evil" was all about. To her, it was just the "tree in the middle of the garden."

She **added** to it. She said something God never said: "You must not touch it." She made it more sinister than it was. That led her to avoid it, which wasn't what God desired. He wanted her to understand what this test meant.

She **subtracted** from it. Eve eliminated an important part of God's command. God had said that if she ate, she would "surely die." But Eve put it this way: "lest you die" (KJV). She made it sound possible that she might not die.

She **erased** part of it. God had said she could eat "freely" (Genesis 2:16) from all the other trees. But Eve left out the word "freely" (in the original). In other words, she diminished God's goodness. She made Him sound like a skinflint.

What was the result? Eve played right into the devil's hands. He knew when she misquoted God's Word that she not only didn't understand it and couldn't apply it, but she also didn't respect it enough to learn it properly. As a result, she and Adam fell.

How about you? Is that how you treat the Word of God?

THE EXTRA MILE

How are we to treat God's Word?

Read these texts. What do they say about how we use God's Word?

Psalm 1:1-3
Matthew 5:17-19
2 Timothy 2:15
2 Timothy 3:16-17
Psalm 119:11

Tuesday:

Why Does God Test Us?

Todd Chambers paused at the water fountain in the school corridor and bent to get a drink. He slurped several quick mouthfuls of water, then straightened up to head to class. He felt jittery and afraid. If he didn't pass this geometry test, he might flunk the whole course. The thought of another summer of remedial classes made him feel sick.

He steadied himself and hurried down the hall. He'd studied, given it his best shot. When the teacher passed out the questions, Todd's heart sank. The first two befuddled him. He wondered if he was simply stupid. His forehead felt hot as he gazed around at the rest of the students bent over their papers.

He worked along as best he could. When he turned in the test, though, he knew it was hopeless. As he walked out of the classroom, he murmured, "Why does everything have to be so hard, God?"

Though he was a Christian, at times he felt as though God had deserted him. He sat quietly on the bus that night, fighting an impulse to swear. His mind buzzed with anger. "Why don't You make things work out?" he asked God again as he walked home alone. But there was no answer, and his frustration only mounted.

Tests in school can be horrible. Tests in life can be worse. God often allows us to go through difficult circumstances for months and even years without solution. Which of us hasn't asked, "Why doesn't God do something?"

We find the answer when we understand why God allows us to be tested and put through grueling mental and physical circumstances. Here's an acrostic that might help: the P-U-R-P-O-S-E of God's tests.

To **produce** obedience (Hebrews 5:8). When we are tested, we learn to obey, even when it hurts.

To **urge** dependence on God (1 Corinthians 12:9-10). Stout tests usually make us want to get closer to God, even if we're angry with Him.

To **ready** us for future work (Philippians 2:5-8). A football coach puts a team through hard testing to get them ready for the real trial on the gridiron.

To **perfect** us (James 1:2-4). Testing is God's

way of maturing us.

To **overcome** sins and problems (1 Peter 4:12-10). Testing cleanses. It teaches us to change and live for Him.

To **sharpen** us (1 Peter 5:9, Proverbs 17:17). Just as iron sharpens iron, so testing makes us stronger, more resilient, better equipped.

To **expose** weaknesses (Luke 22:31-34). God desires to show us where we're weak.

Indeed, testing makes us more like Jesus. For that reason, we can welcome it and struggle through it with determination.

THE EXTRA MILE

Look up the verses above and comment on each one as it relates to testing.

Wednesday:

Using God's Word against the Devil

When Jesus faced Satan in the wilderness, the devil pulled no punches. He hurled everything he had at the Lord.

Jesus responded to each of Satan's taunts, lies and temptations with the words, "It is written." He parried the assaults with Scripture. It's an important lesson. Jesus demonstrates to us that the Scriptures are a potent sword and weapon against the devil.

Consider the P-O-W-E-R of God's Word.

1. It **provides** authority. So many people struggle with the choices of life. They're not sure what's right, what's wrong and what's up to them. Scripture rids us of that problem. Much of sin can be dealt with simply by knowing what God says and obeying it.

2. It **organizes** your thinking. The devil loves to confuse us. Once confused, we're easy toys he can manipulate to his own ends. But as we meditate on and use Scripture, it helps us think ever more clearly. Many Bible teachers even recommend memorization of the Word as a way to get better grades. Why does it work? Because it sharpens our minds, makes us better thinkers and teaches us to concentrate.

3. It **withstands** assault. Doubt often leads to desertion. When we're not sure what God says, we certainly can't obey Him. But when we know His Word on an issue, we know His will and command. That can help us withstand the devil's lies.

4. It **ends** argument. Ever argue with the devil? Who usually wins? The devil is the best debater in history. Don't argue with him. Quote the Word. Obey it. Apply it to your situation. It terminates all further discussion.

5. It **reinforces** you in your convictions. There's something comforting and encouraging about quoting the Word of God out loud. As we quote it, we find that it makes us feel stronger, better able to face the rips of the enemy.

During World War II, Winston Churchill rallied

the people of Great Britain with his blood-stirring words: "We will fight on the beaches . . . We will fight in the hills . . . We will never surrender." Those carefully framed words emboldened the people and made them believe they could stop Adolph Hitler.

In the same way, God gives us His Word in vibrant golden flames of hope. It empowers us. Have you ever gone through the "valley of the shadow of death" (Psalm 23:4) without remembering "the LORD is my shepherd" (23:1)? Have you ever felt spiritually hungry and turned to Jesus' words, "I am the bread of life" (John 6:35)? Or dragged in tired and beaten down and turned to "Come to me, all you who are weary and burdened" (Matthew 11:28)?

Words have power. God's Word has God's power. Use it and you will stand.

THE EXTRA MILE

Study these passages for more insight into the power of God's Word:

Psalm 119:105
Romans 15:4
1 Corinthians 10:11-13
2 Peter 1:20-21

Thursday:

Bait

Ever wonder what a fish thinks when he sees a fat worm hanging off a razor-thin hook? Maybe something like, "Yo, Mama!" Or, "Catch a load of that honey!"

Fishing is a common and graphic image used frequently in Scripture. It's the classic means of deceit. Hold out a delectable dish and the fish will get hooked.

The devil uses similar tactics on all of us. He hangs his bait, throws out his line and waits for us to bite. As we study Scripture, we can see in the temptation of Eve and also of Jesus in the wilderness that Satan follows a clear strategy for catching his dinner. Consider several typical steps:

1. *A possibility.* The first thing that happens is we become aware of a possible action. Steal some money. Smoke marijuana. Engage in illicit sex. We realize we can pull it off. Or so we think.

2. *A hunger for this possibility.* In stage two we begin "lusting" after that sinful thing. We want it. We hunger for it, think about it, dream about it. Soon it's something on our minds all day.

3. *Rationalization of Scripture.* The third step is to rid our minds of fear about that sin. How? By

telling ourselves Scripture says nothing about it. Or that our interpretation of the Bible on that point is wrong. We convince ourselves it isn't wrong to do such and such.

4. *Compromise of Scripture.* In this stage, we decide that even though the Word commands us to avoid this sin, we'll do it anyway. We compromise our beliefs.

5. *Experimentation.* Next, we might experiment. Try a little here and there. Nothing too big. Just enough to find out what it's like.

6. *Giving in.* Once we like what we see, we begin engaging in it regularly. We develop the habit of sinning.

7. *Sell-out.* At this point, we're close even to giving up our walk with Christ. We just don't care anymore.

What do we do? There are two ways to go: *confession of sin* or *rebellion.* We're all capable of going either way.

Do you find yourself in this slip and slide into sin? Why not stop now and confess it before it's too late?

THE EXTRA MILE
Take a look at how these folks in Scripture dealt with sin. Can you see how each step must have been taken?

Ananias and Sapphira in Acts 5:1-11
Peter in Galatians 2:11-13
King Saul in 1 Samuel 15:1-25

Friday:

Escape!

One of my favorite movies is called *The Great Escape*. In it a band of prisoners of war during World War II manages to pull off a daring mass escape from a POW camp. They tunnel underground for over 300 feet, then come up in a field near a wood. How they do it is carefully chronicled. Each step becomes a mini-drama in which one or more men risk to accomplish their goals.

In the end, most of the escapees are caught and shot. We feel outrage. Yet, what we see through it all is the burning desire of men to be free, to get out of their cages, to find the way through their troubles so that they can breathe free and easy.

One of God's great promises about escaping from temptation is found in First Corinthians 10:13. In that passage we see the ingredients of God's "escape hatch" for tempted Christians.

What does the Scripture teach?

First, that we're no different from each other. "No temptation has seized you except what is common to man." All of us experience the same temptations. No one is unique. No one is immune. No one can say, "I've been going through something no one since the beginning of time has faced." No, we're all in the same boat.

Second, Paul says we're to rely on God's faithfulness. Paul asserts, "God is faithful." How so? In two ways:

1. He *limits temptation*. God "will not let you be tempted beyond what you can bear." In other words, God sets bounds for the devil. That's a rather sobering truth. It means we can't excuse ourselves when we sin. We can't say, "It was more than I could bear." Or, "It was just too much." No, the Lord assures us it's never that way.

2. Paul also says that God *leads us through temptation*. He will "not let you be tempted beyond what you can bear," but will "also provide a way out." God builds an escape hatch into every temptation we face. If we simply look for it, we will discover the devil really doesn't have the upper hand.

What are some routes of escape? Running is one. Just getting out of there. Resisting is another. Fighting back. You might also try singing and rejoicing. Some Christians find that a song seems to get their mind off the power of a line of temptation. For every temptation we face, God provides a way out, a way up, a way down or a way through. We can count on it.

THE EXTRA MILE

Look at these passages and identify the way Scripture says we might escape temptation:

2 Timothy 2:22
James 4:6
Acts 16:26
Daniel 1:8-14
Psalm 3:1-2, then 3-4

Weekend:

Don't Give Up

The Rose Bowl in 1929 was quite a show. The University of California battled Georgia Tech valiantly, and just before the end of the second quarter a fumble occurred that might have changed the game. Roy Riegels, a UC defensive player, picked up the ball and ran for the goal line.

The wrong goal line. One of his teammates tackled him just a few yards before scoring a touchdown for Georgia Tech. When UC took over, they were backed to the wall. Ultimately they gave up a safety. Two points.

With Georgia Tech now ahead, UC filed into the locker room. Roy Riegels slumped down in a corner, put his head on his knees and sobbed. Nibbs Price, UC's coach, was very quiet as was the rest of the locker room. No one seemed to know what to say or do. Obviously, part of the coach's problem was what members of the team to play in the second half. Would he let Roy Riegels go back in?

With only minutes left in half time, Nibbs Price suddenly said, "Men, the same team that played the first half will start the second."

All the players filed out, except one. Roy Riegels still sat in the corner, his eyes full of tears, his shoulders hunched. The coach called to him, "Riegels!"

The broken player didn't move.

Nibbs Price walked over to Roy and said, "Roy, didn't you hear me? I said, 'The same team that played the first half will start the second.'"

Roy slowly turned to his coach. He looked shattered, but the coach waited for his reply. "Coach," he said, "I can't do it. I've ruined you. I've ruined the University of California. I've ruined myself. I couldn't face that crowd in the stadium to save my life."

The coach didn't hesitate. Gripping Roy's shoulder, Coach Price said, "Roy, get up and go on back; the game is only half over."

Riegels suddenly realizing all his coach was saying, stood and ran out. It was said that no one had ever seen him play as hard and well as he did that second half. Even though UC lost, in that single act of forgiveness and support, Nibbs Price probably accomplished more than all the piled-up statistics on the playing field. A man was redeemed.

Like Roy Riegels, God forgives us when we sin—over and over, forever. There is no sin He cannot forgive, and ultimately no sin that can fell us. God gives us second, third, hundredth and

thousandth chances. Whatever we need to succeed.

If you recall nothing else from this book,
remember this: there is no sin God can't forgive if
we turn to Him in faith.

God will forgive. Simply ask. Confess your
failure and let Him speak to your heart. You can
lose ground. You can lose blessings. You can
even lose great hopes. But you can't lose Jesus,
or His love.

THE EXTRA MILE

Read these passages on God's forgiveness and
consider what they say about how God forgives
us:

Isaiah 44:22
Isaiah 35:17
Isaiah 43:25
Micah 7:19
Psalm 103:12
Matthew 6:13-14
1 John 1:9

CHAPTER 6

Showing Others the Way

Monday:

God's Goals

What is God's most heartfelt desire?

Paul gives us an indication in First Timothy 2:3-4: "This is good, and pleases God our Savior, who wants all men to be saved and to come to a knowledge of the truth."

Dwight Moody, great evangelist of the nineteenth century, felt an urgency to preach the gospel to as many people as he could. He said, "I look on this world as a wrecked vessel. God has given me a lifeboat and said to me, 'Moody, save all you can.' This world is getting darker and darker; its ruin is coming nearer and nearer. If you have any friends on this wreck unsaved, you had better lose no time in getting them off."

Leading friends and family to Christ is often the most difficult and frustrating part of being a Christian. Here, you have come to a knowledge of all these wonderful truths. You know you're headed for heaven. You're convinced that Jesus is the Savior of the world, the Lord of the universe. And yet, most people you know and meet do not agree. They have their own beliefs, and who are you to tamper with them?

God does want all people to be saved. His fervent desire is that none of us perish. But He also knows that many will reject the truth till the day they die.

The way He intends to fulfill the Great Commission to tell the gospel to every person on earth is through personal evangelism–you and me going to our neighbors, coworkers and fellow students, and telling them what we have discovered. God's goal is nothing less than the complete conversion of the planet.

A battle rages every day between the powers of good and evil. Satan and his cohorts fight on trying to prevent believers from sharing the gospel and unbelievers from accepting it. God and His angels war against the devil and carve out paths for Christians to trek everywhere they can. It's a constant struggle, and we're in the middle of it.

C.T. Studd, a famed missionary of the last century who left riches and sure fame in England as a cricket player, said, "Some wish to live within the sound of church or chapel bell. I want to run a rescue shop within a yard of hell."

There are few things in life more inspiring than to lead a friend to Christ. To reach that point takes courage, determination, prayer and faith. Ask yourself: do I want to be a signpost to heaven? Can I take the message to others?

The answer to the second question is yes. Anyone can take the message. Paul was a tentmaker. Peter worked as a fisherman. Matthew gathered taxes and was hated by hundreds of his countrymen. But God chose them and used them mightily to take His message to a dead world.

He can use you, too. If you will let Him.

THE EXTRA MILE

Read Christ's primary message to His disciples about His plan in Matthew 28:18-20. What do you see in this passage as Jesus' main concerns in the process of winning the world? What parts of it are you now doing? What parts would you like to begin doing?

Tuesday:

What Is Evangelism?

One of Aesop's fables tells of an argument between the sun and the wind. Each said it was stronger than the other and they agreed to a duel. They spotted a traveler wearing a coat and both decided that whichever one could make him take off his coat the soonest was the more powerful.

The wind went first and blew a mighty blast at the man, fierce as a Mediterranean storm. But with each blast, the traveler simply pulled his coat closer about him and bent into the wind, determined not to lose his one source of warmth. Failing after many tries, the wind gave up and the sun went to work. He slathered the traveler in bursts of warm beams. Very soon the man cheered up, unbuttoned his coat and finally took it off. The sun was declared the winner.

Aesop then makes his point: "It has always been believed that persuasion is better than force. The sunshine of a kind and gentle attitude will sooner open a man's heart than all the bluster and power of a tyrant."

If evangelism is anything, it is persuading a person to open his heart to Christ through kind and gentle words, love, goodness and character.

Evangelism means going out into the highways and byways of life and speaking to people about the Savior who has come, died for their sins and risen again that they might live.

Romans 10:13-15 gives a helpful picture of the process. There Paul says,

> "Everyone who calls on the name of the Lord will be saved."
>
> How, then, can they call on the one they have not believed in? And how can they believe in the one of whom they have not heard? And how can they hear without someone preaching to them? And how can they preach unless they are sent? As it is written, "How beautiful are the feet of those who bring good news!"

Notice the progression:

- Call on Christ
- Believe in Christ
- Hear the message
- Send the preacher

If you reverse it, you have a good picture of the process of evangelism:

- Send
- Hear

- Believe
- Call

That is evangelism: go with the message, tell it to the hearer, hope that they will believe and ultimately persuade them to call on the name of Christ.

It's not a difficult method to use. Anyone who wants to can learn to do it effectively.

THE EXTRA MILE

Read through Romans 10:1-15. What do you see in this passage about Paul's heart and his concern for the lost? What steps or parts of it have you already engaged in? What parts would you like to become involved with?

Wednesday:

Telling Your Story

Dr. Tony Campolo has encouraged thousands of students with his speaking, wit and humor. I once heard him talk about how to do evangelism effectively. He dealt with some of the objections that people have to doing evangelism:

You say, "I don't know how." What do you need to know? Or you say, "I don't have style." Who has style? Nobody has style. Listen–if you were on the great ship Titanic and you saw water gushing into the hull of the ship and you ran up to the top deck, what would you do? Say, "Oh, I would like to tell people that the ship is sinking, but I'm not really prepared for things like this. They were running a seminar at my church, *Ten Ways to Tell Someone the Ship Is Sinking*, but I was busy on that night and I didn't make it to the meetings."

Come on–the urgency of the situation compels you to tell people the good news. I know guys who stutter and stammer and who can't get out a line. But they're married. Which means that somewhere along the line they communicated something to somebody!

One of the best ways to communicate the gospel is to simply tell what you know. Like the person above, no one needs a seminar on ten ways to tell others the ship is sinking. All you need to do is run up to the top deck and start yelling.

A powerful way to share the gospel is to tell your story. Just tell people what happened to you, how you changed, what Christ has done in your life, all that has happened since you took that step. Some call it "giving your testimony" and it's the simplest thing in the world, just as we all like to tell stories about who did what at school and how Uncle Hal ran out of gas on the freeway and what a great game it was when Bill Muggs slammed that double in the bottom of the ninth with bases loaded and two outs. We all tell stories naturally. It doesn't take a gift. In a way, it's just talking to the neighbor across the fence.

How do you give a testimony?

1. Tell what you were like before you became a Christian.
2. Tell how you became a Christian.
3. Tell what's happened since you took that step.

In fact, you don't have to follow this process. You don't have to think in terms of steps. Just tell what happened to you.

How do you get started? Ask a question: "Can I tell you about something great that happened to me?" Or, "Hey, listen to this. Something incredible happened to me and I've got to tell everybody." Let it slip into the give and take of normal conversation.

"How ya doing, Chuck?"

"Pretty good. You?"

"Not bad. Anything up these days?"

"Not really."

"Well, let me tell you something that happened to me . . ."

If you're worried about the way people respond–will they reject you, or mock you, or laugh?–remember Satan stokes that fear. It's his primary weapon in keeping Christians from telling others the good news. Take the risk and step out. The way God works will surprise you.

THE EXTRA MILE

See how Paul tells his story in Acts 26:2-23. What elements of personal testimony do you see in Paul's speech? How would you tell your story under such circumstances?

Thursday:

Telling the Story

There is another story to tell besides your own, and that is *the* story of Christ's coming, life, death and resurrection. Strangely, many people do not know many of the details of Jesus' life. They know little of who He was, what He came to do and where He is now. They may know a few facts, that Christianity is based on Jesus' teachings and so on, but often that's as far as it goes. Frequently, their understanding of Jesus is colored by whatever religious experiences they had as a child.

Often, *the* story is best told in bits and pieces– sharing a thought here and there, some little insight you've gotten in your quiet time. Often, though, a way to tell *the* story is by telling a little part of your story.

Tell them something that happened to you–an answer to prayer, a strange "coincidence" that smacks of God's power, a special gift that came out of nowhere.

Open the conversation in such a way that you can tell the story of Christ.

How do you tell the story?

1. Make people aware of your beliefs about Christ through telling about what happened to you. Don't keep things to yourself. If someone else can tell you how much they enjoyed the ballgame last night, why can't you tell them about the great sermon you heard on Sunday–or something else?

2. Foster an image of being open and willing to talk about religious things, without being pushy. Cultivate the image that you're a Christian and open to their questions and needs.

3. Pray that God will open the hearts of people around you and that they will respond to your stories and friendship.

4. Share things about your faith naturally, as part of the conversation. Don't feel you have to force it, though, if it doesn't fit.

What most people don't like is Christians who butt into their "space" and determine to tell them about Christ against their will. Jesus is best shared in an open, tolerant, friendly atmosphere than in a confrontational, cold, buttonhole situation.

THE EXTRA MILE

Look how Peter tells the story in Acts 2:14-39. How does he use the opportunity presented? What does he spell out for his listeners? How do you think you would have reacted to his preaching if you had been there?

Friday:

Answering Objections

Becky Pippert, an author of books on evangelism and a traveling speaker, relates a story of a conversation with a professor while on an airplane. He asked what kind of work she did, and she explained about InterVarsity Christian Fellowship. As she spoke, she spotted that subtle shift in his eyes that indicated he thought she must be some nut. But Becky found a way to break through the haze. When she finished, the professor said in a stilted way, "I'm sure it must be . . . ah . . . very rewarding."

Becky answered, "Well, I'm not sure it's as rewarding as it is intriguing."

She goes on, "Almost in spite of himself he said, 'How do you mean, intriguing?' "

She responded, "I think one of the hardest issues a Christian must face is how in the world we know that what we believe is true. How do we know we are not deluding ourselves and worshiping merely on the basis of need rather than truth? Or that Freud is not correct in saying we worship a glorified version of our father-figure? To have to deal honestly with those questions is exciting and intriguing.

"He looked at me in surprise and said, 'You

won't believe this but those are the very questions I have. Well, how do you know it's true?'

"For the rest of our flight," she writes, "we discussed the evidences for the Christian faith."[9]

How do you answer objections to the faith? You will find that once you get a chance to tell your story or *the* story, people will raise all kinds of objections, from why there are hypocrites in the church, to whether there's really a hell, to how could a good and loving God permit evil. Like the example above, it often takes some subtlety and salesmanship to crack through the facade. But there are ways we nonprofessionals can learn to share our faith without stumbling all over ourselves when unbelievers pin us to the wall with a stout objection.

For one thing, be honest. Don't fake it. If you don't have an answer, don't pretend you do by hiding it in highfalutin' speech. Non-Christians respect honesty more than professorial answers anyway.

Second, when you get an objection, think it through before you do answer. If you need some time–a few days to study up–request it. "Can I get back to you on that?" God doesn't have to save someone on the spot!

Third, take time to begin learning answers to questions unbelievers ask. Amazingly enough, there are only about twelve different questions asked in ninety-five percent of all cases. Evangelists and preachers who have written books on the subject repeatedly find that the same questions are asked over and over in conversations about faith and Christ.

Fourth, ask the Lord to guide. He will give you ideas as you talk. Learn to ask intriguing questions yourself. Don't be afraid to challenge an opinion.

Fifth, remember you don't have to convert a person on the spot. Many people need time to think over an answer. You could be talking to some friends over a period of years before they'll actually think about trusting Christ. So think of each situation as a chance to plant a seed.

THE EXTRA MILE

Look at how Jesus answered a woman's objections in John 4:1-26. How did He approach her? How was He different from other people? How did He keep the woman to the main issue?

Weekend:

Praying for Your Friends

William Carey, missionary to India, worked for seven years before he saw a single convert to Christian faith. Adoniram Judson labored in Burma also for seven years before anyone began to follow Christ. He told his supporters back in England, "Beg the churches to have patience. If a ship were here to carry me to any part of the world, I would not leave my field. Tell the brethren success is as certain as the promise of a faithful God can make it."

Missionaries in New Zealand witnessed for over nine years before the first convert was baptized. Believers in West Africa struggled on for 14 years before seeing any fruit. And in Tahiti, workers prayed and evangelized for 16 years before the first Christian convert was counted.

One of my friends, a young pastor, always gives this advice to men and women bent on winning the world for Christ: "Preach, pray and plug away."

Plug away, preach and pray. That's the name of the game. Remember what it took to bring you to Christ. Undoubtedly many people prayed for your salvation before it actually happened. So why should it be any different for your friends? They need time and prayer, too.

What can you pray for?

- That God will give you oppor-tunities to share the gospel.
- That God will open their hearts.
- That God will allow you to show something of Christian faith and character in action so that Christ is made attractive to them.
- That God will give you oppor-tunities to love and serve.

John Wesley used to say, "Preach as if everything depended on you, and pray as if everything depended on God."

That's good advice. Ask God to make you an agile, potent witness to the truth. Pray that He leads you to become persuasive, able to answer objections, and ready for anything that might arise in a witnessing situation. Pray that He opens your heart to real service and love.

A doctor with a heavy schedule wanted to lead his neighbor to Christ. He saw the man out in his backyard one day, planting little clumps of grass so that a lawn might eventually grow. The doctor had some free time so he walked over to offer his neighbor help. Soon, the two men got that lawn in shape.

Later, that doctor decided to start a home Bible study for people in his neighborhood. He invited the man next door. That man brought twenty-seven other neighbors with him to the study! Service and love have an impact!

Pray that God will give you opportunities to love, serve and show off the character of Christ. That will speak whole volumes to your friends that all your witnessing can't equal.

THE EXTRA MILE

Look at Paul's attitude in prayer about those who were lost in Romans 10:1-2. What does this passage show you about his love and desire to help his people?

Monday:

Planting Seeds

Some Christians approach evangelism as a one-time, one-chance effort. You meet someone in the elevator, you give him or her a tract, share a few thoughts and run. You're going door to door and just trying to interest a person enough to let you lead him through a method you've learned, maybe Evangelism Explosion, the Four Spiritual Laws or some other succinct, simple statement of the gospel. Or you're in the line at the supermarket and suddenly you find yourself in a conversation with one of the patrons about your faith.

A close friend of mine was converted while hitchhiking one day. He got a ride and the driver turned out to be a Christian. My friend eventually prayed to become a Christian through that man's witness.

Another man I know turned on television one day and there was a Billy Graham Crusade on the station. He listened and decided to receive Christ–right there in his underwear!

However, these are unusual cases. The kind of evangelism that really changes lives is often through Christians in steady, regular contact with unbelievers. Most people who accept Christ accept Him through the witness of a friend, relative, fellow worker, or someone else who has consistent contact with them. Few believers come to faith through a one-time, one-opportunity chance experience with a fervent evangelist.

Lewis C. Hohenstein said, "If the world and our communities are to be evangelized, it will not be through great sermons, good teachers, or good TV and radio programs. It will be accomplished because there are living examples of Christians and Christian families among unbelievers everywhere. The greatest evangelistic force that the world will ever know is the force of Christian families who live in peace, joy and respect for one another in a chaotic world."

Think in terms of planting seeds everywhere you go. What I mean by "seeds" are little pointers to Christ. Any story, comment, thought or shared moment that includes the truth of Christ counts. Maybe it's a short testimony of a prayer answered. Perhaps you received a great insight from a radio broadcast you listened to. Maybe it's a chance to pray before a meal. Or maybe a friend has poured out his or her heart to you about some personal struggle and you offer to pray for them. Maybe it was just a great day that you could thank God for. It can be anything, really–anything that points to the fact that you believe in a God who is there and who shares our pain, eases our burdens and promises good in the midst of evil.

Share those moments with those you love. Tell them about that prayer. Do it humbly. Do it in a friendly way. Don't push yourself on them. You will find that many people who aren't open to a whole gospel presentation will listen with interest to your anecdotes, stories and thoughts.

I cut out a little poem in *Decision* magazine, written by a man named Jim Hancock. It's always been a thought-provoking picture to me of real evangelism. Hancock wrote,

> I was
> Armed against argument,
> Ready for rhetoric,
> Loaded for logic,
> But I had
> No defense against love.[10]

Plant those seeds in love and watch them grow.

THE EXTRA MILE

Read Jesus' parable about the sower in Matthew 13:1-9, 18-23. What does this passage reveal about planting seeds? What are the different kinds of responses that a seed-planter gets? Have you seen those responses in those you've tried to reach? How and where?

Tuesday:

The Personal Touch

A pastor spoke with one of the young men who came regularly to hear him preach. He said, "I hope you're a Christian."

The young man replied, "No, I am not a Christian, but I know you and have heard you preach for seven years."

The pastor immediately took the young man aside and spoke with him heart to heart. In less than a half hour, the young man decided to accept Christ.

After getting married, a non-Christian bride and her new husband decided to live with his parents for a while to give themselves a happy start on life. It was only a short time later that she became a Christian. When asked why, she said, "One could not live in that home very long with its love for the Lord without becoming a Christian."

It's personal involvement that speaks so powerfully to those who don't know Jesus. Jesus received Nicodemus late at night and answered his questions kindly but firmly. When Jesus stood at the well in Sychar and spoke with the woman who had had five husbands, He again was gentle but straightforward and personal. He didn't give her a list; He gave her a taste of His heart.

When the friends of the paralyzed man let him down through the roof of the house where Jesus was teaching, again Jesus got personal. The first thing He said to the man was, "Son, your sins are forgiven" (Mark 2:5b). When Jesus first met Andrew in John 1, He invited him to come to His house and "see" whether He was truly the "Lamb of God" as John the Baptist had said. And when Andrew introduced Jesus to his brother Simon, Jesus gave Simon a new name: Peter, which means "rock." In all these situations, the personal element won people to Christ. It will work that way for you as well.

How do you use the personal touch?

1. Learn to listen. Ask questions. Find out about this person you would like to tell the gospel to. Find out who they are, and tell them about yourself–the good and the bad.

2. Share your life with them. Invite them to your house, or to a concert or a party. Whatever seems to you to be the best way to befriend them. Let them know you care.

3. Be available. Tough times strike every life. There are moments of weakness, fear and worry for all of us. It's at those times when we should be most ready to love, to serve, to listen, to help–not just to thrust the gospel down their throats. Maybe that's not even the best time to do that. But to build the relationship so at other times, when they're thinking more clearly, they can indeed listen–that is what you're working toward.

Years ago, a man in Indianapolis was struggling with many of the questions of faith. In the same town, a layman heard of his struggles and went to visit. He opened the conversation with a statement. "Tell me about all the problems you're having with the Scriptures. Perhaps I can help you with them."

The doubter poured out his questions and soon the two embarked on a fervent, intense conversation. In the end, every objection answered, the layman said, "Will you kneel with me as I pray for you now?" After prayer, he asked the man if he'd like to accept Christ as Savior. He did. Later the layman told his pastor, "I've enjoyed many thrilling things in my life, but this experience outranks them all."

That layman was Benjamin Harrison, who had in earlier years served as twenty-third president of the United States.

The personal touch. It wins friends, influences people and can be a means to leading the lost into fellowship with Christ.

THE EXTRA MILE

Study how Jesus used the personal touch with Nicodemus in John 3. What principles do you see at work in the meeting? How did Jesus reach out to this important but confused leader?

Wednesday:

Being Tolerant

The marketplace of opinion overflows with new and old ideas. Even in high schools in modern America you will find Christians are a minority. You will meet Roman Catholics, Jehovah's Witnesses, Mormons, Jews, Muslims, Buddhists, Hindus, atheists, agnostics and Christian Scientists, to name only a few of the different groups out there. Many of those believers are articulate and can put a Christian to shame with their ability to defend their faith.

What is a godly outlook in such an atmosphere?

Above all, you want to remember that just as we Christians believe we have the truth, so most people involved in other faiths "believe" they have the truth, too. Sometimes they will say something like, "You have your truth and I have mine. Your truth is true for you, and so is mine. So why can't we just be friends?" Sometimes just being friends will open a door that "forcing" them to hear your gospel won't.

Consider, too, that many of the non-Christians you meet are just as sincere in their beliefs as you are in yours. Sincerity doesn't make one truer than another. But it does make the case that much harder. Missionaries say that the hardest groups to convert are those most entrenched in their traditional religion.

In talking to people of other persuasions, you might consider four ways of relating to them. First, don't attack and condemn. Even Jesus rarely condemned anyone. He never attacked the Romans for their idolatry or the Samaritans for their rejection of true Judaism. Rather, He found "common ground" that He used as a point of departure to lead them closer to the kingdom. The woman at the well is a good example of this outlook (see John 4).

Second, give them a chance to tell you their story. You may find that they have some real questions that their own faith has failed to answer. If you listen, they might reveal genuine doubt. It's at those points that your personal testimony can be very powerful.

Third, pray and plant seeds. Befriend them. Be open. Share your home and your life with them. It will speak far more than trouncing arguments that simply anger them.

Fourth, give God time to work. The conversion of people ingrained in other faiths often takes years of work and effort. Don't expect the battle to be won in a day or a week.

Ultimately, though, there is great hope. An article in a Christian magazine spoke of Patrick Sookhdeo of Guyana, at one time a committed Muslim who became a Christian. He was approached by a group of Free Church Christians who befriended him. In time, they discussed religion. Patrick found he was intellectually superior to them and often won arguments. But inwardly, even as he was winning points in debate, he thought, "There is more in these people than there is in me." That emptiness and need for fulfillment led him to seek Christ.[11]

It can happen the same way for you and your religious friends.

THE EXTRA MILE

Look at two contrasting ways men of faith have dealt with those of other faiths.

1 Kings 19:1-46
Acts 10:23-48

Thursday:

Letting Them Make Their Own Choices

The summer after I graduated from college, I became a Christian. I visited my alma mater in upstate New York intent on leading all my friends back at Colgate University to the Lord. I was full of fervor, faith and strong conviction that God could and would work.

One of the first days back, I found one of my friends, a girl named Leslie, in the arts center. We talked for a few minutes, and suddenly she said to me, "You're different." I said, "What do you mean?" She answered, "You seem like you're at peace, like you're no longer struggling."

I told her about my conversion. She was cordial, but noncommittal. I promised to keep in touch.

From there, I stopped by a sociology class. There we discussed what young people are looking for today. I was with another friend named Ralph and I raised my hand. The prof called on me, and I said, "I think what most young people are looking for today is the truth. They just want to know the truth about life, the world, heaven, hell. All that."

The prof eyed me and said, "What is truth?"

I answered, "That's the same question Pontius Pilate asked Jesus when the governor was about to send Him to the cross."

"And what did Jesus answer?"

I said, "He didn't answer anything."

The prof smiled. "So what is truth?"

I had a Bible in my hand and I held it up. "This." Some of the other students snickered and the prof simply shook his head. "I don't think it's that simple." Then he turned to the class. "What is truth? It is relative. What is true for you might not be true for me, and vice versa. Truth is what you make of it."

I was saddened by that answer. But what could I do? I had already disturbed the class enough. I wasn't even an enrolled student.

That weekend opened my eyes. I found that

many of my friends were not nearly as eager to hear the gospel as I was to present it. Some told me they were offended at my "condescending" manner, saying I acted like I had arrived and they hadn't. I didn't mean to act that way, but my desire that they know Christ was just bubbling out of me like a geyser.

In the process of years of witnessing, sharing, helping others and seeking to win the world for Christ, I have become convinced of an important truth: you have to give each person the time and respect to decide for himself. You cannot force anyone into the kingdom of God. No one ever came to genuine faith in Jesus at the point of a gun.

As you seek to win your friends, relatives and neighbors to faith in Christ, give them the right to make their own decisions. There is a time to tell the story and a time to let it rest. After you've made the gospel as clear as you can, give them a break. Plan B is to live out the faith before them. You may find that they'll be a great deal more interested when they've seen you live it in the tough and tumble of life than in any other way.

THE EXTRA MILE

Look at Jesus' way of dealing with the multitudes who left Him in John 6:66-71. And also how Paul dealt with the rejecters in Acts 13:44-52.

Friday:

What If I Fail?

What if, after all is said and done, you've been living the life before a friend's eyes, you've tried to communicate the gospel, and you've continued to pray for them and love them the best you can–and in the end, they just decide it's not for them? Have you failed?

There are many reasons God might have for putting you and this friend together at this time. Perhaps He wants you to plant the seeds necessary to bear the full fruit years from now. You're just one in a long line of Christian people who will touch this friend's life. There are some Christians who pray for a friend or a relative for years. Some even die before they see their friend saved. But in the end it happens. Just like that thief on the cross. At the last minute, God steps in and the miracle happens.

A second reason this friend is in your life is for you. God is producing in you the fruit of the Spirit in ways you may not even see. He builds gentleness as you edge around the subject. You learn to be tolerant, understanding and sympathetic. He stitches into your life the threads of humility and kindness so essential to reaching other hurting, broken people. He kindles within you a fire of faithfulness that gives you the determination to hang in there even though things aren't going well. God will use this friend to develop you as a person and as a Christian in ways you may not realize until the very end of time.

A third reason God has brought you together is for the others who will observe and assess your friendship. Others watch as you relate to this unbelieving friend. Perhaps they will see in your interaction something that draws them to Christ, or helps them live more faithful, God-honoring lives.

Ultimately, though, it's possible this friend will leave this life without having ever made a statement of faith in Christ. What do you do then?

I have a friend who recently lost her father. She prayed for that man and loved him ever since she became a Christian. But her dad rejected her faith and her Christ. I spoke with her over the phone and she wept as she told me of his death without Christ. "I have no help for him, no hope at all. And he was my own father. Why didn't God bring him to Christ, Mark? Why?"

No one can answer that question. I know theology. I know there's a hell. I know unbelievers go there. But I also know God is merciful, compassionate, loving, holy and all-powerful.

I don't understand why some people believe and others do not. I don't know all the ins and outs of doctrines like election and predestination and so on. But I have put my own trust in the God who is good and loving, "not wanting anyone to perish, but everyone to come to repentance" (2 Peter 3:9b).

That is a confidence worth having.

THE EXTRA MILE

Read Jesus' words in Mark 10:23-31. What does this passage say about those who do not believe? Is there anything that God can do?

Weekend:

No Other Plan

There is an old story about Jesus' return to heaven and His first meeting with the angels. They reel in shock as they see His wounds and learn of the trial of the cross. But they are glad He is alive again and has returned to be with them. The angel Gabriel decides to question Jesus about all that has happened. He says, "Master, You must have suffered for men terribly down there."

"I did," He answers.

"And," continues Gabriel, "do they know all about how You loved them and what You did for them?"

"Oh, no," says Jesus, "not yet. Right now only a handful of people in Jerusalem know."

Gabriel is astonished. "Then what have You done," he asks, "to let everyone know about

Your love for them?"

Jesus says, "I've asked Peter, James, John and a few more friends to tell other people about Me. Those who are told will in turn tell still other people about Me, and My story will be spread to the farthest reaches of the globe. Ultimately, all of mankind will have heard about My life and what I have done."

Gabriel appears skeptical and frowns unhappily. He knows what men and women down there are like. He says, "Yes, but what if Peter and James and John grow weary? What if the people who come after them forget? What if way down in the twentieth century, people just don't tell others about You? Haven't You made any other plans?"

Jesus answered, "I haven't made any other plans. I'm counting on them."[12]

God's plan is you and me—all of us working together to let the world know the truth. Let's each do our part and we'll get there.

THE EXTRA MILE

Read Jesus' last words to the church before His ascension in Acts 1:1-11. What can you begin doing today in light of these words?

It's a Marathon

The Christian life isn't a 100-yard dash; it's a marathon.

There will be days when nothing goes right in your life. And there will be other times when everything you touch turns to gold.

This little journey we've taken has hopefully moved you ahead a few miles on that road.

One of my favorite movies of all time is *Chariots of Fire*. It's the story of Eric Liddell, a Scotsman who ran in the 1924 Olympics and won a gold medal. It is not his victory, however, but the story behind it which shows a unique kind of courage. His best event was the 100-meter sprint, and he was favored to win that event. But the trial heats for the event were on a Sunday. Eric was a Christian and he believed in keeping the Sabbath holy, as the fourth commandment said. He refused to run.

His story made international headlines. Few understood, even some Christians.

But Eric made his stand. He bowed out of the 100 meters and began preparing for another race which wasn't his best event: the 400 meters.

Every Olympics has its riveting, magic moments. In 1968, it was Jean-Claude Killy taking the gold in all three major Alpine skiing events. In 1972, it was Mark Spitz winning seven gold medals in swimming, the only time that has ever happened. In 1980, it was the United States' triumph over the Russian hockey team. In 1924, it was Eric Liddell.

The "flying Scotsman," as he was called, possessed an inimitable, no-holds-barred, all-out running style that thrilled his audience. When he ran a race, toward the end he always threw his head back–not even looking at the course anymore–and his hands flailed in the air like two disconnected live power cables. It was a thrilling, joyous, almost worshipfully raucous style. No one could be certain who would win Liddell's race, either. Others were favored over him. And this wasn't Eric's best event. But as if God chose then and there to reward him for his stand on the Sabbath, Liddell won. The music cranks up as he finishes, and in the movie it's a magic moment.

But there was another moment that I found even more moving in the movie. It was on that harrowing Sabbath when Eric was invited to read the Scripture and preach at a Scottish church in another part of Paris. While this was pure movie myth-making, the picture is a powerful portrait of God's ways against man's. Eric reads from Isaiah 40:28-31, and as he does his words are punctuated by shots from the Olympic stadium where it's raining and men slip, slide and fall into the mud in failure and frustration.

It's always been a favorite passage of mine. Read it now and hear the prophet himself proclaiming these words to tired, broken, lost Israel. Perhaps in them you will hear the voice of God and drink its power.

> Do you not know?
>   Have you not heard?
> The LORD is the everlasting God,
>   the Creator of the ends of the earth.
> He will not grow tired or weary,
>   and his understanding no one can
>   fathom.
> He gives strength to the weary
>   and increases the power of the weak.
> Even youths grow tired and weary,
>   and young men stumble and fall;
> but those who hope in the LORD

will renew their strength.
They will soar on wings like eagles;
they will run and not grow weary,
they will walk and not be faint.

It's a powerful word to those of us who are still running. Moreover, it's a great promise from the Lord who rules.

Meditate on it. Claim it. Use it. Love it.

It's the Word of a Gentleman of the Highest Order, and it can never be broken.

FOOTNOTES

Chapter 1

1. Richard Lyon Morgan, "The Book We Came Back To," *Christianity Today*, March 19, 1982, p. 32.

Chapter 3

2. Dick Eastman, *No Easy Road: Inspirational Thoughts on Prayer*, (Grand Rapids, MI: Baker, 1973), p. 91.

3. Frank Gifford and Charles Mangel, *Gifford On Courage*, (New York: M. Evans and Company, Inc., 1976), pp. 30-31.

4. Eastman, p. 55.

5. Ibid., p. 49.

Chapter 4

6. Beverley Moritz, "One Verse," *Moody Monthly*, April 1981, p. 41.

7. Virginia Stem Owens, "Christianity: Harmlessly Homogeneous with Culture," *Christianity Today*, November 6, 1981, pp. 50-51.

Chapter 5

8. Series of untitled articles in *Young Salvationist*, January-December 1990, p. 15.

Chapter 6

9. Rebecca Manly Pippert, *Out of the Saltshaker and into the World* (Downers Grove, IL: Inter-Varsity Press), pp. 127-128.

10. Jim Hancock, utitled poem, *Decision*, February 1978, back inside cover.

11. Richard Bewes, "What Rocks Ardent Unbelievers," *Eternity*, September 1983, p. 67.

12. Joseph C. Aldrich, *Life-Style Evangelism* (Portland, OR: Multnomah Press, 1981), pp. 15-16.